Elements of the Law of Contract

2000–2001 LLB Examination Questions
and Suggested Solutions

University of London
External Examinations

Solutions by Edwin Lichtenstein
BA, LLB, LLM

OLD BAILEY PRESS

OLD BAILEY PRESS
at Holborn College, Woolwich Road,
Charlton, London, SE7 8LN

First Published 2002

Examination Questions © The University of London 2000
and 2001

Solutions © The HLT Group Ltd 2002

ISBN 1 85836 480 9

British Library Cataloguing-in-Publication.
A CIP Catalogue record for this book is available from the
British Library.

Printed and bound in Great Britain

Contents

Acknowledgement

The questions used are taken from the University of London LLB (External) Degree examination papers and our thanks are extended to the University of London for the kind permission which has been given to us to use and publish the questions.

Caveat

The answers given are not approved or sanctioned by the University of London and are entirely our responsibility.

They are not intended as 'Model Answers', but rather as Suggested Solutions.

The answers have two fundamental purposes, namely:

a) to provide a detailed example of a suggested solution to examination questions, and
b) to assist students with their research into the subject and to further their understanding and appreciation of the subject.

Note

Please note that the solutions in this book were written in the year 2002. They were appropriate solutions at the time of preparation, but students must note that certain case law and statutes may subsequently have changed.

Introduction

Why choose Old Bailey Press publications?

In addition to providing students with a comprehensive, accessible range of study materials in the form of our Integrated Student Law Library, Old Bailey Press continues to ensure that students can maximise their potential in examinations with our series of Suggested Solutions. Our range of Textbooks, 150 Leading Cases, Cracknell's Statute Books and revision aids provide students with an invaluable collection of affordable reference books which will be of assistance from the very beginning of their course right through to the examinations themselves.

Suggested Solutions

The Suggested Solutions series provides examples of full answers to real examination papers. The solutions contained in this book go beyond what would reasonably be expected of a candidate under examination conditions. The opportunity has been taken, where appropriate, to develop themes, suggest alternatives and set out additional material providing further comprehensive topical coverage, making them an excellent addition to the conscientious student's study materials.

We feel that in writing full opinion answers we can assist you with your research and further your understanding and appreciation of the law. It must, however, be recognised that at this level of study there is almost certainly more than only one approach to any examination question.

Notes on examination technique

Although the substance and slant of any answer alters according to the subject matter of the question, the examining body and the syllabus concerned, the technique required to answer examination questions well does not change.

It is impossible to pass an examination if you do not know the substance of a course. You will only have a slim chance of passing an examination if you have not grasped the technique required for answering a question. In order to do well in your examinations you must learn, and practice, the technique of answering problems correctly. The following is a guide intended to help you acquire that technique.

Time
One of the most daunting aspects of examinations is the imposition of a strict time limit, during which you must answer a set number of questions. Each question will carry a certain number of marks, and it is imperative that you give each question the appropriate period of time for the marks that it carries. It goes without saying that you should not spend an hour answering a 5 mark question and half an hour answering a 20 mark question. If all

questions carry equal marks, give them an equal amount of time and attention. Do not be tempted to overrun on a question simply because it is going well.

Reading the question
It will not be often that you will be able to answer every question on an examination paper. Inevitably, there will be some areas in which you feel better prepared than others. You will prefer to answer the questions which deal with those areas, but you will not be able to judge which questions are the best ones for you to answer unless you read the whole examination paper.

You should spend at least ten minutes at the beginning of the examination reading the questions. Preferably, you should read them more than once. As you go through each question, make a brief note on the examination paper of any relevant cases and/or statutes that occur to you even if you think you may not answer that question: you may well be grateful for this note towards the end of the examination when you are tired and your memory begins to fail.

Re-reading the answers
Ideally, you should allow time to re-read your answers. This is rarely a pleasant process, but will ensure that you do not make any silly mistakes such as leaving out a 'not' when the negative is vital. It is very easy to make silly mistakes when writing quickly and under pressure: a re-reading of your answers should help you to spot and correct these errors.

The structure of the answer
Almost all examination problems raise more than one legal issue that you are required to deal with. Your answer should ideally do the following.

Identify the issues raised by the question
This is of crucial importance and gives shape to the whole answer. It indicates to the examiner that you appreciate what he is asking you about.

This is at least as important as actually answering the questions of law raised by that issue. The issues should be identified in the first paragraph of the answer.

Deal with those issues one by one as they arise in the course of the problem
This, of course, is the substance of the answer and where study and revision pay off.

If the answer to an issue turns on a provision of a statute, cite that provision briefly, but do not quote it from any statute you may be permitted to bring into the examination hall
Having cited the provision, show how it is relevant to the question.

If there is no statute, or the meaning of the statute has been interpreted by the courts, cite the relevant cases
'Citing cases' does not mean writing down the name of every case that happens to deal with the general topic with which you are concerned and then detailing all the facts you can think of.

You should cite only the most relevant cases – there may perhaps only be one. No more facts should be stated than are absolutely essential to establish the relevance of the case. If there is a relevant case, but you cannot remember its name, it is sufficient to refer to it as 'one decided case'.

Whenever a statute or case is cited, the title of statute or the name of the case should be underlined
This makes the examiner's job much easier because he can see at a glance whether the relevant material has been dealt with, and it will make him more disposed in your favour.

Having dealt with the relevant issues, summarise your conclusions in such a way that you answer the question
A question will often ask you to advise one or more parties. The advice will usually turn on the individual answers to a number of issues. The point made here is that the final paragraph should pull those individual answers together and actually give the advice required. For example, it may begin something like: 'The effect of the answer to the issues raised by this question is that one's advice to A is …'.

Related to the previous paragraph, make sure at the end that you have answered the question
For example, if the question says 'Advise A', make sure that is what your answer does. If you are required to advise more than one party, make sure that you have dealt with all the parties that you are required to and no more.

Some general points
You should always try to placate the examiner and win him round to your way of thinking. One method has already been mentioned – the underlining of case names, etc. There are also other ways in which you can do this.

Always write as neatly as you can. This is more easily done with ink than with a ball-point. Avoid the use of violently coloured ink eg turquoise; this makes a paper difficult to read. Space out your answers sensibly: leave a line between paragraphs. You can always ask for more paper. At the same time, try not to use so much paper that your answer book looks too formidable to mark. This is a question of personal judgment.

Finally, never put in irrelevant material simply to show that you are clever. Irrelevance is not a virtue, and time spent on it is time lost for other, relevant, answers.

Examination Paper

University of London

LLB Examination June 2000

Elements of the Law of Contract

Zone A Examination Paper

Time allowed: **three** hours.
Answer **four** of the following **eight** questions.

1. On Monday, A telephoned B and left a message on B's answering machine offering to sell B his sports car for £10,000. B's wife telephoned A, saying that B was away for two weeks. A said he would wait for B's return before doing anything else. B's wife said, 'Good! I promise to inform B as soon as he returns.' On Wednesday, by letter A offered to sell his car to C. On Thursday C posted a reply stating, 'I'll buy it at that price. Is it green?' C's letter was delayed in the post till Saturday. Meanwhile on Friday, B returned earlier than expected, and e-mailed A agreeing to buy the car for £10,000. A replied by e-mail, 'Yes! It is yours.' B did not receive this e-mail till Sunday.

   Advise the parties of their contractual position.

2. 'When one or more parties to a contract are mistaken it is not always easy to advise about the remedies which are available.'

   Discuss.

3. D, who was deaf, went to an auction run by E. D had a copy of the catalogue and had intended to bid for a picture attributed to Lowry. When the lot came up, E explained that there was some doubt about the authenticity of the picture and that E could not guarantee that it was genuine. However, D did not hear this qualification and bought the picture for £26,000. An expert later confirmed that it was probably a very good copy worth £3,500. D sought to return the painting and recover compensation. The conditions of sale which were posted on the walls of the auction rooms stated,

   > 'There is no warranty about the condition of goods. Goods sold subject to errors of description.'

   Advise D. What difference, if any, would it make to your advice if D were an art dealer who had bought the painting to sell on in the course of D's business?

4. G went to H's shipyard explaining that he needed a boat to realise his life's ambition to travel round the world. G was sold 'Jenny', a 42 foot boat for £40,000. It was a type suitable for world touring. G spent the remainder of his life savings to stock the boat with considerable quantities of provisions. G engaged J to survey the boat and he gave it a clean bill of health. Three months later G set out on his circumnavigation of the world.

3

Three days into the Atlantic Ocean the boat developed a severe leak and G had to put about. The boat was found to be unsound and in need of considerable expenditure to make her seaworthy.

Advise G. What difference, if any, would it make to your advice if the contract between J and G had limited J's liability to the contract fee of £300?

5. 'Payment of a sum less than that due does not discharge the original contractual obligation. This is why the courts have gone to extraordinary lengths to provide the person who has paid the lesser sum with some form of protection. But this protection is heavily circumscribed.'

Discuss.

6. K was a licensed dealer in gaudy china under the (fictitious) Antiques Dealers Act 2000. Section 1 of the Act prohibits dispositions of gaudy china by dealers without a licence. According to s2 of the Act all dispositions have to be accompanied by a statutory notice describing the goods, stating the quantity and indicating the price.

K sold and delivered two gaudy cups and saucers to L. They were described as Aberdare pattern but the statutory notice failed to state the agreed price of £200.

K sold and delivered a gaudy bowl to M for £400. However, K did not deliver a statutory notice after M had said that he did not need one.

K sold and delivered two gaudy jugs to N for £600. K supplied a statutory notice two days after delivery. Subsequently, N discovered that one of the jugs had been repaired and wanted to return the two jugs to K.

K sold and delivered two gaudy teapots to P for £800 with a statutory notice but unknown to K his licence under the Act had expired.

Advise K. K has not been paid for any of the china expect by N who has paid £600 in advance.

7. On Monday, R, agreed to sell her car to S for £6,000 after he had represented that he was the well known sports personality T. S asked R to accept a cheque but R refused. S produced an identification card with T's name on it below S's photograph. R rang up the number S gave and an accomplice answered and the accomplice misrepresented S's identity. R went to the library and checked that T lived at the address given.

R eventually allowed S to take the car in return for a cheque supposedly drawn on T's account. On Wednesday, it was dishonoured. On learning of this, R contacted the police and the local garages. On Thursday, S sold the car to X for £3,000. S cannot be traced.

Advise the parties.

8. 'It remains unsatisfactory that the law is unclear about when an innocent party can bring a contract to an end for breach, especially as damages are often uncertain or difficult to quantify.'

Discuss.

Suggested Solutions

Question One

On Monday, A telephoned B and left a message on B's answering machine offering to sell B his sports car for £10,000. B's wife telephoned A, saying that B was away for two weeks. A said he would wait for B's return before doing anything else. B's wife said, 'Good! I promise to inform B as soon as he returns.' On Wednesday, by letter A offered to sell his car to C. On Thursday C posted a reply stating, 'I'll buy it at that price. Is it green?' C's letter was delayed in the post till Saturday. Meanwhile on Friday, B returned earlier than expected, and e-mailed A agreeing to buy the car for £10,000. A replied by e-mail, 'Yes! It is yours.' B did not receive this e-mail till Sunday.

Advise the parties of their contractual position.

Suggested Solution

General Comment

This is a reasonably straightforward question on offer and acceptance.

Skeleton Solution

A's offer to B: when and if it was communicated; the effect of the promise to keep it open – A's offer to C: C's reply; an acceptance or a counter-offer?; if an acceptance, the application of the postal rule – the exchange of e-mails between A and B.

Suggested Solution

A's offer to B was left on B's answering machine. Clearly the offer was not communicated at that stage. Whilst there is no clear authority on the communication of messages on telephone answering machines, it appears from *Entores Limited* v *Miles Far East Corporation* (1) that an *acceptance* on the telephone is only communicated when it is actually heard, and it is submitted that this should also apply to an offer. Moreover, there is nothing to suggest that B's wife had authority to act on his behalf.

A undertook, in effect, to keep the offer open until B's return. It is trite law that an offer can be revoked at any time before acceptance: *Routledge* v *Grant* (2). In the absence of consideration, A's promise to keep the offer open could not be enforced.

We are informed that, on the Wednesday, A made a further offer to sell the car to C. What has to be considered is whether C's reply constituted an acceptance of that offer and, if it did, when that acceptance was communicated.

C's reply is not, on the face of it, an unconditional acceptance of the offer, in view of the query as to the colour of the car. If this query constitutes the introduction of a new term, then C's letter is a counter-offer, which of course destroys the original offer: *Hyde* v *Wrench* (3). However, it can be argued that C's reply is a conditional acceptance, the condition being satisfied if the car is in fact green. Moreover, it could well be that the query 'Is it green?' is no more than a request for information, which in no way invalidates A's offer: *Stevenson* v *McLean* (4). On either of the above constructions there has been an acceptance by C of A's offer.

The next question is whether this acceptance has been communicated: this involves consideration of the postal rule. It was established in *Adams* v *Lindsell* (5) that when the postal rule applies, communication is deemed to have been effected when the letter of acceptance is posted. In *Henthorn* v *Fraser* (6) Lord Herschell stated that the postal rule would apply, in the absence of contrary indications, where the offer has been made by post, which is the situation here. The fact that the letter of acceptance is delayed in the post does not negate the application of the postal rule: *Household Fire Insurance Co* v *Grant* (7).

It seems, therefore, that as there was a valid acceptance and that this was effectively communicated, a contract between A and C was concluded on the Thursday.

It remains to consider the position as between A and B.

A has, in fact, purported to revoke his offer to B by his subsequent negotiations with C. But whilst, as stated above, an offer can be revoked at any time before acceptance the revocation must be actually communicated before the acceptance has, or been deemed to have, been communicated: *Byrne & Co* v *Van Tienhoven & Co* (8). On the Friday A's offer to B has presumably been communicated, and B, being unaware of any revocation, purports to accept it. He does so by e-mail. Whilst it could have been suggested that A, having made the offer by telephone, expected an acceptance by the same medium, this is contradicted by A having replied by e-mail. In any event it is submitted that, as A has not prescribed any particular form of acceptance, an e-mail is equally efficacious: *Tinn* v *Hoffman & Co* (9); *Manchester Diocesan Council for Education* v *Commercial & General Investments Ltd* (10).

I have made the assumption that A's offer was still open when B sent his e-mail. If, for some reason, this were not so, then B's e-mail would have constituted the offer, which A then accepted by the same method. It is unnecessary to consider whether an acceptance by e-mail is deemed to be communicated when it is sent, or only when it is received, as B actually receives the e-mail on the Sunday, at which time he is totally unaware of the contract with C.

The somewhat untidy conclusion is, therefore, that A has concluded contracts with both of the other parties. As C's contract was concluded on the Thursday he has the prior right, and might conceivably have a claim for specific performance. B would be limited to a claim for damages for breach of contract.

References

(1)   [1955] 2 QB 327
(2)   (1828) 4 Bing 653
(3)   (1840) 3 Beav 334
(4)   (1880) 5 QBD 346
(5)   (1818) 1 B & Ald 681
(6)   [1892] 2 Ch 27

References (contd.)

(7)   (1879) 4 Ex D 216
(8)   (1880) 5 CPD 344
(9)   (1873) 29 LT 271
(10)   [1970] 1 WLR 241

Question Two

'When one or more parties to a contract are mistaken it is not always easy to advise about the remedies which are available.'

Discuss.

Suggested Solution

General Comment

This is a somewhat wide-ranging question. Whilst the main issue is the doctrine of mistake, there are situations in which, although a party entered into a contact under a mistake, that mistake will not operate to make the contract void at common law, or render it liable to be set aside in equity. This involves consideration of the law relating to misrepresentation and the remedies for breach of contract.

Skeleton Solution

Mistake at common law: the general rule; the effect of operative mistake, when the mistake renders the contract void; types of mistake – mistake in equity: when the mistake renders the contract liable to be set aside in equity – situations where the mistake neither makes the contract void, nor renders it voidable in equity – possible remedies for misrepresentation or for breach of contract.

Suggested Solution

Mistake at common law

The general rule is that mistake does not affect the validity of a contract: *Smith v Hughes* (1). There are, however, situations where a mistake will render the contract void at common law. The types of mistake that can occur are: where one party is mistaken (unilateral mistake); where the parties are at cross purposes (sometimes referred to as mutual or bilateral mistake); or where the parties share the same mistake (common mistake).

'If mistake operates at all, it operates so as to negative or in some case to nullify consent': per Lord Atkin in *Bell* v *Lever Brothers Ltd* (2).

The fact that one party is (unilaterally) mistaken as to the terms of the contract will only affect its validity in exceptional circumstances as in *Hartog v Colin & Shields* (3).

One party may be mistaken as to the identity of the other party. Where the contract is concluded inter praesentes that mistake will not usually negative consent and thus render the contract void: *Phillips v Brooks Ltd* (4); *Lewis v Averay* (5); but see *Ingram v Little* (6).

10

Where the parties are dealing with each other at a distance the situation may be different, if it appears that the intention was only to deal with a particular, designated person: *Boulton v Jones* (7); *Cundy v Lindsay* (8).

Where mistake as to identity does not render the contract void, the injured party may have an action for misrepresentation. This is dealt with further below.

Mistake may negative consent, thus rendering the contract void, where the parties are at cross purposes (mutual or bilateral mistake): *Scriven Bros & Co v Hindley & Co* (9); *Raffles v Wichelhaus* (10).

In the case of common (shared) mistake, the mistake may operate so as to nullify consent and render the contract void. But the operation of common mistake at common law was confined to very narrow limits by the decision in *Bell v Lever Brothers Ltd* (above). Mistake may so operate in exceptional circumstances, such as purchasing one's own property: *Cooper v Phibbs* (11). Common mistake may also have this effect where the mistake is as to the existence of the subject matter: s6 Sale of Goods Act 1979: *Couturier v Hastie* (12). But a party may not be able to rely on a mistake if he had no reasonable ground for that belief: *McRae v Commonwealth Disposals Commission* (13).

A somewhat difficult question is whether a mistake as to the quality of the subject matter can render a contract void. It did not do so in *Bell v Lever Brothers Ltd*. But it is theoretically possible: see the propositions enunciated by Steyn J in *Associated Japanese Bank Ltd v Credit du Nord SA* (14).

Where a common mistake does not make contract void at law, it may render it voidable – liable to be set aside – in equity. The leading authority in this regard is *Solle v Butcher* (15)* This decision was followed in *Grist v Bailey* (16) and *Laurence v Lexcourt Holdings Ltd* (17), although the correctness of these two decisions was doubted by Hoffmann LJ in *William Sindall plc v Cambridgeshire County Council* (18).

This equitable remedy of rescission is discretionary, and is not usually available for unilateral mistake, unless the party against whom it is sought has been at fault: *Riverlate Properties Ltd v Paul* (19). In the case of unilateral mistake equity may operate to the extent of refusing an order for specific performance to the party seeking to enforce the contract: *Malins v Freeman* (20).

It remains to consider the position where, although a party is mistaken, the mistake does not operate to make the contract either void or voidable.

The mistake may have been induced by a misrepresentation which induced the injured party to enter into the contract. Here the equitable remedy of rescission may be available, that is rescission for misrepresentation, not for mistake. Thus where one party misrepresents his identity, the innocent party may seek to have the relevant contract set aside.

In addition, the innocent party may be entitled to damages. If the misrepresentation is fraudulent, the innocent party will be entitled to damages for the tort of deceit. Even if the misrepresentation was not fraudulent he may be entitled to damages under s2(1) Misrepresentation Act 1967.

It may be that the false statement is not a 'mere' representation, but is a term of the contract. In that event the remedy will lie in an action for breach of contract. The precise remedy will depend on the nature of the term that has been breached. If the term is a warranty (or treated as such) the remedy will lie in damages. If the term is a condition (or treated as such) the innocent party will be entitled, in addition to a claim for damages, to treat the breach as a repudiation of the contract.

Note: This appears to be no longer correct. In the Court of Appeal in *Great Peace Shipping Limited* v *Tsavliris (International) Limited* in a judgment dated 14 October 2002 ((2002) The Times 17 October) Lord Phillips MR, delivering the judgment of the Court, said:

'In this case we have heard full argument, which has provided what we believe has been the first opportunity in this court for a full and mature consideration of the relation between *Bell* v *Lever Brothers Limited* and *Solle* v *Butcher*. In the light of that consideration we can see no way that *Solle* v *Butcher* can stand with *Bell* v *Lever Brothers Limited*. In these circumstances we can see no option but so to hold.'

References

(1)   (1871) LR 6 QB 597
(2)   [1932] AC 161
(3)   [1939] 3 All ER 566
(4)   [1919] 2 KB 243
(5)   [1972] 1 QB 198
(6)   [1961] 1 QB 31
(7)   (1857) 2 H & N 564
(8)   (1878) 3 App Cas 459
(9)   [1913] 3 KB 564
(10)   (1864) 2 H & C 906
(11)   (1867) LR 2 HL 149
(12)   (1856) 5 HL Cas 673
(13)   (1951) 84 CLR 377
(14)   [1988] 3 All ER 902
(15)   [1950] 1 KB 671
(16)   [1967] Ch 532
(17)   [1978] 1 WLR 1128
(18)   [1994] 3 All ER 932
(19)   [1975] Ch 133
(20)   (1837) 2 Keen 25

Question Three

D, who was deaf, went to an auction run by E. D had a copy of the catalogue and had intended to bid for a picture attributed to Lowry. When the lot came up, E explained that there was some doubt about the authenticity of the picture and that E could not guarantee that it was genuine. However, D did not hear this qualification and bought the picture for £26,000. An expert later confirmed that it was probably a very good copy worth £3,500. D sought to return the painting and recover compensation. The conditions of sale which were posted on the walls of the auction rooms stated,

> 'There is no warranty about the condition of goods. Goods sold subject to errors of description.'

Advise D. What difference, if any, would it make to your advice if D were an art dealer who had bought the painting to sell on in the course of D's business?

Suggested Solution

General Comment

Discussion of different possibilities is required here: the statement in the catalogue, whether it is a contractual term or a representation; the effect of E's explanation; the effectiveness of the exclusion clause; and the consequence of D having dealt in the course of business.

Skeleton Solution

On the assumption that the statement in the catalogue is a contractual term, the possible breach of s13 Sale of Goods Act 1979, the effect of the exclusion clause where D is dealing as a consumer and in the course of business – on the assumption that the statement is a representation, the question of inducement and the effect of the exclusion clause.

Suggested Solution

I shall firstly consider the possibility that the statement attributing the picture to Lowry is a term of the contract. The first question is whether the sale of the painting falls within s13(1) Sale of Goods Act 1979 as being a 'sale of goods by description', it being an implied term (a condition) that the goods correspond with the description.

In order for a sale to fall within s13, the description must relate to the identity of the goods sold: *Reardon Smith Line Ltd* v *Hangsen-Tangen* (1). Clearly that requirement is satisfied. There is, however, a further requirement, it must have been reasonable for the buyer to have relied on the description: *Harlingdon & Leinster Enterprises Ltd* v

Christopher Hull Fine Art Ltd (2). This creates a difficulty for D. The auctioneer, E, stated the doubt about the authenticity of the picture. (I consider the fact that D did did not hear this explanation, because he was deaf, irrelevant.) In the light of this explanation and the notice posted on the walls of the auction rooms, I submit that it would not have been reasonable for D to have relied on the description and that accordingly s13(1) does not apply. A fortiori this conclusion would be justified if D had bought the picture in the course of business.

Nevertheless, I should consider the possibility that the sale was one by description within s13, and the effect of the exclusion clause in that event. It may well be that, applying the contra profenterem rule, the clause does not cover the breach: it purports to exclude a *warranty*, whereas the breach is of a *condition*: *Wallis, Son & Wells* v *Pratt & Haynes* (3). If it does cover the breach, then the provisions of the Unfair Contract Terms Act 1977 are relevant. If D was dealing as a consumer, then under s6(2) of that Act the clause would be void. If D was dealing in the course of business then under s6(3) it would have to meet the requirement of reasonableness. In view of E's explanation it seems that it might do so.

However, I have concluded that the attribution of the picture was not a contractual term. There is a further reason for doing so. The paramount factor in determining whether a statement is to be construed as a term is the intention of the parties: *Heilbut, Symons & Co* v *Buckleton* (4). Clearly there was no such intention.

Although the statement attributing the painting to Lowry was not a term, it appears that it did amount to a representation and, being false, constituted a misrepresentation. It was clearly a statement of fact and addressed to D (amongst others). Did it induce D to enter into the contract? There is room for doubt about this in view of E's explanation (which I have assumed D should have heard). The question is one of onus of proof. Whilst the statement might not, in view of E's explanation, have induced a reasonable man to enter into the contract, D could argue that it did induce him; the onus of proof would be on D: *Museprime Properties Ltd* v *Adhill Properties Ltd* (5). He would succeed in establishing inducement if he discharged that onus. I assume, although not without doubt, that he could do so. This might be more difficult for him if he was an art dealer.

Assuming that there was an actionable misrepresentation, further consideration must be given to the exclusion clause. This clause refers to 'warranty' and 'description' and does not expressly refer to a representation. Arguably it therefore does not apply. If it does, its effectiveness must be considered in the light of s3 Misrepresentation Act 1967, as amended by s8(1) Unfair Contract Terms Act 1997. Under this provision the clause would be of no effect unless it satisfied the requirement of reasonableness stated in s11(1) of the latter statute. Whilst E's explanation might be persuasive that it did so, I shall assume, for the purpose of further discussion, that the clause is ineffective.

It would appear, consequently, that D has an action for misrepresentation and the remedies available to him must now be considered.

D wishes to return the painting, thus seeking the equitable remedy of recission. He appears to be entitled to this. There do not appear to be any of the bars to rescission. Before 1967 the performance of the contract would have been a bar because of the doctrine in *Seddon* v *North Eastern Salt Co* (6), but that bar was removed by s1 Misrepresentation Act

1967. There is no suggestion of the other bars applying, such as affirmation, impossibility of restitution, third party rights or delay.

Under s2(2) Misrepresentation Act 1967 the court has a discretion to award damages in lieu of rescission, but there is insufficient information to determine whether or not a court would exercise that discretion.

D also seeks compensation. No information is given as to the loss he might have sustained that would not compensated for by his being able to rescind. If he has sustained other loss, then his entitlement to damages must be briefly considered.

If the representation were fraudulent D would be entitled to damages for the tort of deceit. But there are no grounds for assuming fraud here. However, even in the absence of fraud, D would be entitled to damages under s2(1) Misrepresentation Act 1967 unless the representor proves both that he believed that the attribution of the picture was true and that he had reasonable grounds for that belief. It is difficult to see how that onus could be discharged. The measure of damages under s2(1) is the same as for fraud: *Royscott Trust Ltd* v *Rogerson* (7).

References

(1)   [1976] 1 WLR 989
(2)   [1990] 3 WLR 13
(3)   [1911] AC 394
(4)   [1913] AC 30
(5)   [1990] 36 EG 114
(6)   [1905] 1 Ch 326
(7)   [1991] 3 All ER 294

Question Four

G went to H's shipyard explaining that he needed a boat to realise his life's ambition to travel round the world. G was sold 'Jenny', a 42 foot boat for £40,000. It was a type suitable for world touring. G spent the remainder of his life savings to stock the boat with considerable quantities of provisions. G engaged J to survey the boat and he gave it a clean bill of health. Three months later G set out on his circumnavigation of the world. Three days into the Atlantic Ocean the boat developed a severe leak and G had to put about. The boat was found to be unsound and in need of considerable expenditure to make her seaworthy.

Advise G. What difference, if any, would it make to your advice if the contract between J and G had limited J's liability to the contract fee of £300?

Suggested Solution

General Comment

The consequences of two contracts have to be discussed here. The contract between G and H was one for the sale of goods and requires discussion of the possible breach (or breaches) and the remedies available to G. The contract between J and G was a contract for services, again requiring discussion of the possible breach: in this latter contract the effect of the limitation clause will have to be examined.

Skeleton Solution

G's contract with H
Defining the contract – sale of goods, application of s14 Sale of Goods Act 1979 – nature of the breach – remedies, rejection of the boat? – damages, measure of and the question of remoteness of damage.

G's contract with J
Definition of the contract as one for the supply of services – application of s13 Supply of Goods and Services Act 1982 – effect of the limitation clause.

Suggested Solution

G's contract with H
The contract is one for the sale of goods. As H, the seller, sold the boat in the course of business the provisions of s14 Sale of Goods Act 1979 apply. Under s14(2) there is the implied condition that the goods were of satisfactory quality. As G explained the particular purpose for which he required the boat, s14(3) applies, under which there is the implied

16

condition that it was reasonably fit for that purpose. There appear to be clear breaches of both these subsections, (It is assumed that these defects existed at the time of the sale, otherwise there would be little to discuss in this regard.)

The primary remedy for the buyer for breach of a condition under the Sale of Goods Act 1979 is rejection of the goods. However, in this instance G will be deemed to have accepted the boat under s35 of the Act by the delay and his use of the boat, and by virtue of s11(4) the breaches can only be treated as breaches of warranty. This limits G to a claim for damages.

In respect of the boat itself the measure of damages is provided for by s53(3) of the Act as being the difference between the value of the boat at the time of delivery and the value it would have had if it had fulfilled the terms of s14.

It also appears that G had spent a considerable sum stocking the boat with provisions. It is not made clear to what extent this sum has been lost but it is assumed that there has been some loss in this regard. This raises the question of remoteness of damage.

The rule stated in *Hadley* v *Baxendale* (1) is that damages:

> ' … should be such as may fairly and reasonably be considered either arising naturally, that is, according to the usual course of things, from such breach of contract itself, or such as may reasonably be supposed to have been in the contemplation of both parties at the time they made the contract as the probable result of the breach of it.'

For further discussion and application of this rule: see, inter alia, *Victoria Laundry (Windsor) Ltd* v *Newman Industries Ltd* (2) and *The Heron II* (3).

The expenditure incurred by G could not be regarded as arising naturally from the ordinary course of things, the first limb of the rule. But its loss could be said to have been in the reasonable contemplation of the parties as the probable result of the breach, the second limb of the rule. H was made aware that G intended to travel round the world and could have been reasonably expected to have contemplated that this type of expenditure would have been incurred, and would be wasted in the event of the boat being unserviceable. It should be noted that if damage can be contemplated recovery is not limited because the degree of damage could not have been anticipated: *H Parsons (Livestock) Ltd* v *Uttley Ingham & Co Ltd* (4).

G's contract with J

This contract is one for the supply of services. It can be assumed that J, the supplier, was acting in the course of business, and under s13 Supply of Goods and Services Act 1982 there is an implied term that the supplier will carry out the service with reasonable care and skill. J was in breach of that term.

The breach of the implied term by J could only have resulted from his negligence and he will accordingly be liable for all the direct conequences of the breach, unless he can rely on the limitation clause which must now be considered.

This clause purports to limit J's liability to the contract fee of £300. However, under s2(2) Unfair Contract Terms Act 1977, the clause is subject to the requirement of reasonableness. (It is also subject to s3(2)(a) of the Act, which imposes the same requirement.) The reasonableness test is set out in s11(1) and, by s11(5), the onus of proving that the clause satisfies the test falls on J.

It is not possible on the present information to determine whether or not the clause would satisfy the test. Some guidance could be obtained from the speech of Lord Griffiths in *Smith* v *Eric S Bush* (5), where his Lordship stated the matters that should always be considered. These were:

1. The respective bargaining strengths of the parties.
2. Whether there was an alternative source of the advice.
3. The difficulty of the task being undertaken.
4. The practical consequences of the decision: this would require consideration of the ability of the parties to bear the loss involved and the question of insurance.

The application of (4), the practical consequences criterion, would suggest that the clause would not satisfy the reasonableness test, but this must remain a tentative view.

References

(1)   (1854) 9 Exch 341
(2)   [1949] 2 KB 528
(3)   [1969] 1 AC 350
(4)   [1978] QB 791
(5)   [1989] 2 All ER 514

Question Five

'Payment of a sum less than that due does not discharge the original contractual obligation. This is why the courts have gone to extraordinary lengths to provide the person who has paid the lesser sum with some form of protection. But this protection is heavily circumscribed.'
    Discuss.

Suggested Solution

General Comment

This question requires discussion of the common law rules of consideration in relation to the payment of a lesser sum, and the modification of the common law rules by the equitable doctrine of promissory estoppel.

Skeleton Solution

The common law – the rule in *Pinnel's Case* – the origin and development of the doctrine of promissory estoppel – limitations of the doctrine.

Suggested Solution

At common law the rule in *Pinnel's Case* (1) is that 'Payment of a lesser sum on the day in satisfaction of a greater sum cannot be any satisfaction for the whole.' This rule was affirmed by the House of Lords in *Foakes* v *Beer* (2) and more recently by the Court of Appeal in *Re Selectmove Ltd* (3). But even at common law there were certain limitations on the rule, if there was deemed to be accord and satisfaction. Thus, the debt could be discharged by payment in kind, or by earlier payment, or by payment elsewhere: *Couldrey* v *Bartrum* (4); *Vanbergen* v *St Edmunds Properties Ltd* (5). Payment of a lesser sum could also discharge the debt if if were made by a third party: *Hirachand Punamchand* v *Temple* (6).

However, the protection that has been afforded to the person who has paid the lesser sum stems from the development of the equitable doctrine of promissory estoppel. The origin of this doctrine lies in the decision of the House of Lords in *Hughes* v *Metropolitan Railway Co* (7) where Lord Cairns LC stated that it was a clear rule of equity that where one person, by his words or conduct, had led the other party to believe that his strict rights under the contract would not be enforced, or would be held in suspense or abeyance, then that person would not be entitled to enforce those rights where it would be inequitable to allow him to do so. (The earlier, and possibly conflicting, decision of the House of Lords in *Jorden* v *Money* (8) was not quoted.)

In *Hughes* v *Metropolitan Railway Co* the landlord was estopped from claiming the forfeiture of a lease, but the equitable principle was applied by Denning J (as he then was) to the payment of a lesser sum of money in obiter dicta in *Central London Property Trust Ltd* v *High Trees House Ltd* (9). The effect of this development was that where a creditor had promised to accept a lesser sum in discharge of the (larger) debt he could be estopped from claiming the balance. This doctrine of promissory estoppel is in conflict with the decision in *Foakes* v *Beer*, and represents an equitable modification of the common law principle.

The scope and limits of the doctrine of promissory estoppel must now be examined,

First, there must have been a clear and unambiguous promise; it is not sufficient that the creditor merely failed to enforce his contractual rights: *Woodhouse A C Israel Cocoa Ltd SA* v *Nigerian Produce Marketing Ltd* (10).

Second, the doctrine provides 'a shield, not a sword', that is, it operates as a defence, it does not create a cause of action where none existed before: *Combe* v *Combe* (11). (There is a different application of the doctrine by the High Court of Australia in *Walton Stores (Interstate) Ltd* v *Maher* (12).)

Third, the promisee must have relied on the promise, he must have acted on it in some way. It is not entirely clear what this involves. There are obiter dicta to the effect that it is not necessary for the promisee to have acted to his detriment, he must merely have done something he would not otherwise have done: per Denning LJ in *W J Alan & Co Ltd* v *El Nasr Import & Export Co* (13); and per Goff J in *Société Italo-Belge etc* v *Palm Oils etc, The Post Chaser* (14). However, in *Goldsworthy* v *Brickell* (15) Nourse LJ rejected the application of the doctrine because he could find no evidence of detriment.

Fourth, it must be inequitable for the promisor to go back on his promise: see the judgment of Lord Denning MR in *D & C Builders Ltd* v *Rees* (16).

Fifth, it appears that the doctrine operates so as to suspend the creditor's rights, not to extinguish them. The Privy Council in *Ajayi* v *Briscoe* (17) and the House of Lords in *Tool Metal Manufacturing Co Ltd* v *Tungsten Electric Co Ltd* (18) emphasised that the promisor could resile from his promise by giving the other party reasonable notice, allowing him to resume his former position. This represents a curtailment of the doctrine as originally formulated in *High Trees*. But in that case Denning J held the view that the estoppel had permanent effects because the lessors would not have been able to demand the arrear rentals.

To hold that the operation of the doctrine is suspensory is satisfactory where the contractual obligation involves payment by instalments, but less so where it involves a single, lump sum, payment. To hold, however, that the operation of the estoppel can be extinctive would clearly be in conflict with *Foakes* v *Beer*.

Difficulties remain. In *Woodhouse A C Israel Cocoa Ltd* (above) Lord Hailsham LC said:

> 'I desire to add that the time may soon come when the whole sequence of cases based on promissory estoppel since the war beginning with *Central London Property Trust Ltd* v *High Trees House Ltd*, may need to be reviewed and reduced to a coherent body of doctrine. I do not mean to say that any are to be regarded with suspicion. But as is common with an expanding doctrine they do raise problems of coherent exposition which have never been systematically explored.'

The time has still not come.

References

(1)   (1602) 5 Co Rep 117a
(2)   (1884) 9 App Cas 605
(3)   [1995] 2 All ER 531
(4)   (1881) 19 Ch D 394
(5)   [1933] 2 KB 223
(6)   [1911] 2 KB 330
(7)   (1887) 2 App Cas 439
(8)   (1854) 5 HL Cas 185
(9)   [1947] 1 KB 130
(10)   [1972] AC 741
(11)   [1951] 2 KB 215
(12)   (1988) 164 CLR 387
(13)   [1972] 2 QB 189
(14)   [1982] 1 All ER 19
(15)   [1987] 1 All ER 853
(16)   [1966] 2 QB 617
(17)   [1964] 1 WLR 1326
(18)   [1955] 1 WLR 761

Question Six

K was a licensed dealer in gaudy china under the (fictitious) Antiques Dealers Act 2000. Section 1 of the Act prohibits dispositions of gaudy china by dealers without a licence. According to s2 of the Act all dispositions have to be accompanied by a statutory notice describing the goods, stating the quantity and indicating the price.

K sold and delivered two gaudy cups and saucers to L. They were described as Aberdare pattern but the statutory notice failed to state the agreed price of £200.

K sold and delivered a gaudy bowl to M for £400. However, K did not deliver a statutory notice after M had said that he did not need one.

K sold and delivered two gaudy jugs to N for £600. K supplied a statutory notice two days after delivery. Subsequently, N discovered that one of the jugs had been repaired and wanted to return the two jugs to K.

K sold and delivered two gaudy teapots to P for £800 with a statutory notice but unknown to K his licence under the Act had expired.

Advise K. K has not been paid for any of the china expect by N who has paid £600 in advance.

Suggested Solution

General Comment

This area, illegal contracts, has been the frequent subject of a question in recent years. The issue posed is the effect of illegality, the extent to which a guilty and an innocent party can enforce an illegal contract.

Skeleton Solution

In each of K's contracts the purpose of the Act in question will have to be examined as to whether the contract is illegal as formed, or merely illegal in its performance. Does the Act prohibit the contract entirely, or only impose an obligation on one of the parties to it? In this context the requirements of a licence and the furnishing of a statutory notice will have to be considered.

Suggested Solution

In *Phoenix General Insurance Co Greece SA* v *Administration Asigurarilor de Stat* (1) Kerr LJ summarised the position with regard to the statutory control of contracts as follows:

'(i) Where a statute prohibits both parties from concluding or performing a contract when both or either of them have no authority to do so, the contract is impliedly prohibited: see *Re Mahmoud & Ispahani* (2): ...

(ii) But where a statute merely prevents one party from entering into a contract without authority and/or imposes a penalty on him if he does so (ie a unilateral prohibition) it does not follow that the contract itself is impliedly prohibited so as to render it illegal and void.'

This statement of the law will now be applied to each of K's contracts.

The contract with L

The Act has imposed a unilateral obligation on K, with which he has not fully complied. Provided that K did not intend to perform the contract in an illegal manner at the time it was concluded (and this is not suggested) it would appear that he is entitled to enforce it: *St John's Shipping Corporation* v *Joseph Rank Ltd* (3). In *Shaw* v *Groom* (4) a lessor had failed to furnish his tenant with a rent-book as required by the statute but was nevertheless entitled to sue for the rent, because the purpose of the statute was to punish his failure to issue a rent-book, not to invalidate the tenancy agreement. I would be satisfied that K could enforce payment of the purchase price, but the doubt stems from the earlier decision in *Anderson Ltd* v *Daniel* (5) where a seller was denied enforcement because of his failure to issue a statutory notice: he had failed to perform the contract in the only way that it was permitted.

The contract with M

Here it would appear that both parties intended to perform the contract in an illegal manner. In *St John's Shipping Corporation* v *Joseph Rank Ltd* (above) Devlin J said

'... a contract which is entered into with the object of committing an illegal act is unenforceable. The application of this principle depends upon the proof of intent, at the time the contract was made, to break the law; if the intent is mutual the contract is not enforceable at all, and if is unilateral it is unenforceable at the suit of the party who is proved to have it.'

As there does seem to have been this intent at the time the contract was made, K will not be able to enforce the contract, and will be not be entitled to sue for the purchase price.

The contract with N

Here N appears to be an innocent party. There is authority to the effect that such party may be debarred from recovery if he could be found to have 'participated' in the illegal act: *Ashmore, Benson Pease & Co Ltd* v *A V Dawson Ltd* (6). In the absence of evidence to this effect I shall assume that this case does not apply.

It is suggested that there has been a breach of contract by K. Either the goods did not correspond with the description (s13 Sale of Goods Act 1979) or were not of satisfactory quality: s14(2) of that Act.

N is therefore an innocent party who has suffered loss as a result of the breach. It has already been submitted that the purpose of the Act, with regard to the furnishing of the statutory notice, was not to prohibit the disposition of the goods in question, but to control the sellers of such goods. N is therefore able to enforce the contract: *Archbolds (Freightage) Ltd* v *Spanglett Ltd* (7). As the breach was one of a condition (or conditions) N would be entitled to reject the two jugs, and recover his advance payment.

The contract with P

With regard to the requirement of a licence, it is clear that the Act prohibits the disposition of the goods without such licence. K is therefore not able to enforce this particular contract. The fact that he is unaware of its expiry is irrelevant.

I have concluded that K can probably enforce the contract against L, has no defence to the claim by N, and cannot enforce the contracts against M and P. It remains to consider whether K can recover the goods from these two parties as goods transferred under illegal contracts. Property has passed to them: *Singh* v *Ali* (8). The rule in pari delicto potior est conditio defendentis would debar him from doing so. He cannot establish a right without relying on the illegality.

References

(1)   [1987] 2 All ER 152
(2)   [1921] 2 KB 716
(3)   [1957] 1 QB 267
(4)   [1970] 2 QB 504
(5)   [1924] 1 KB 138
(6)   [1973] 2 All ER 856
(7)   [1961] 1 QB 374
(8)   [1960] AC 167

Question Seven

On Monday, R, agreed to sell her car to S for £6,000 after he had represented that he was the well known sports personality T. S asked R to accept a cheque but R refused. S produced an identification card with T's name on it below S's photograph. R rang up the number S gave and an accomplice answered and the accomplice misrepresented S's identity. R went to the library and checked that T lived at the address given.

R eventually allowed S to take the car in return for a cheque supposedly drawn on T's account. On Wednesday, it was dishonoured. On learning of this, R contacted the police and the local garages. On Thursday, S sold the car to X for £3,000. S cannot be traced.

Advise the parties.

Suggested Solution

General Comment

The one issue in this question is mistake as to identity, when it can operate so as to render the contract void and when it will merely render it voidable.

Skeleton Solution

The effect of mistake as to identity, whether the contract is void or voidable – the consequences of the distinction – analysis of the decided cases, and an attempt to derive a principle from those cases.

Suggested Solution

The question at issue here is whether mistake as to identity renders the contract void, or merely voidable. The importance of the distinction is that if the contract is void, it is void ab initio, and no rights can flow from it. If it is merely voidable, an innocent third party might have acquired rights as a consequence of the contract.

I propose to discuss the decided cases in this area of the law, attempt to formulate a principle form those cases, and then apply that principle to the facts before me.

In *Boulton* v *Jones* (1) the basis of the decision was that an offer addressed to a specific named person could not be accepted by another. In *Cundy* v *Lindsay* (2) the finding was that the plaintiff had intended to deal only with a reputable firm of whom the plaintiff knew and not with anyone who might have placed the particular order. In both these cases the contracts were therefore held to be void. (In contrast, in *King's Norton Metal Co Ltd* v *Edridge, Merrett & Co Ltd* (3) the mistake did not have this effect, because the plaintiff could only have intended to deal with the writer of the particular letter, who had fictitiously described himself as trading under the name of a firm which did not in fact exist.)

In the above-mentioned cases the parties were dealing with each other at a distance, which may have been significant. The position might elicit a different approach when the parties are dealing inter praesentes – in each others' presence.

In *Phillips* v *Brooks Ltd* (4) the rogue had misrepresented his identity, and although the shopkeeper had checked that there was a person of that name at the address that was given, the shopkeeper's claim to the goods was defeated by an innocent third party having acquired title to the goods the rogue had obtained by his deception. A similar result ensued in *Lewis* v *Averay* (5). In this case when the rogue, who had misrepresented his identity, proffered a cheque in payment of the car he had bought, the owner of the car requested proof of the claimed identity. Being satisfied by the document then produced the owner parted with possession of the car in return for a worthless cheque. Before the fraud was detected the rogue had sold the car to an innocent third party, whose rights prevailed.

A case which does not accord with the previous two cases is that of *Ingram* v *Little* (6) which also involved the purchase of a car. When the rogue produced a cheque book in order to pay for the car, Miss Ingram had said, in effect, that a cheque was unacceptable and that 'the deal was off'. Thereupon the rogue said that he was a Mr P G M Hutchinson of a certain address. One of Miss Ingram's sisters checked the name and address at a post office and as this was deemed satisfactory, possession of the car was parted with for the worthless cheque. The Court of Appeal, by a majority, held that the contract with the rogue was void. Devlin LJ dissented on the ground that the identity of Hutchinson was immaterial to Miss Ingram, she was only concerned with his creditworthiness. His Lordship also said that where the parties are face to face there is the presumption that the one party intends to deal with the person in front of him. The majority decision in this case is difficult to reconcile with the previous two. A possible explanation is that after initially rejecting a cheque, Miss Ingram only intended to deal with Hutchinson, but this does not bear examination.

It seems therefore that mistake as to identity will only render a contract void where the identity is of crucial importance and where the intention is to deal only with a specific named person. This would explain the decisions which held the contracts void in *Hardman* v *Booth* (7) and *Lake* v *Simmons* (8). It is sometimes said that the distinction is between mistake as to identity and mistake as to attributes. But in *Lewis* v *Averay* Lord Denning rejected this as being a 'distinction without a difference'.

On the present facts it is submitted that *Phillips* v *Brooks Ltd* and *Lewis* v *Averay* must be followed, and accordingly R's mistake does not render the contract void. However, R has been the victim of a fraudulent misrepresentation, and it remains to consider his rights in this regard. The appropriate remedy would be rescission which would enable R to regain possession of the car. But S has sold the car to X. By virtue of s23 Sale of Goods Act 1979 where the seller of goods (S in this instance) has a voidable title to them, but his title has not been avoided at the time of the sale, the buyer (X in this instance) acquires a good title to the goods provided he buys them in good faith and without knowledge of the seller's defect of title. The fact that X bought the car for half the price that S paid might conceivably suggest lack of good faith or that his suspicions should have been aroused but there is no hard evidence to this effect. The remaining question is whether S's title has been avoided before the sale to X.

Notice of rescission should normally be communicated to the other contracting party, but S cannot be traced. R contacted the police and local garages before S sold the car to X. Does this constitute effective rescission and timeously avoid S's title? The facts here are on all fours with those in *Car and Universal Finance Co Ltd* v *Caldwell* (9) where the Court of Appeal held that there had been effective avoidance of title. Applying this case would entitle R to regain possession of the car from X. (It is to be noted that the decision in the above case has been strongly criticised by the Law Reform Committee (10) as going far to destroy the value of s23 Sale of Goods Act 1979.)

References

(1)   (1857) 2 H & N 564
(2)   (1878) 3 App Cas 459
(3)   (1897) 14 TLR 98
(4)   [1919] 2 KB 243
(5)   [1972] 1 QB 198
(6)   [1961] 1 QB 31
(7)   (1863) 1 H & C 803
(8)   [1927] AC 487
(9)   [1965] 1 QB 525
(10)   Twelfth Report (*Transfer of Title to Chattels*), Cmnd 2958, para 16

Question Eight

'It remains unsatisfactory that the law is unclear about when an innocent party can bring a contract to an end for breach, especially as damages are often uncertain or difficult to quantify.'
   Discuss.

Suggested Solution

General Comment

This question requires discussion of two areas of the law: when a contract can be terminated for breach and the quantification of damages. Although obviously related, they are separate areas, each of which would merit a question on its own, and some discussion of quantum of damages has previously been required in Question 4. This makes it somewhat difficult to decide how much of the answer should be devoted to each area.

Skeleton Solution

Remedies for breach of contract: the right to terminate and the entitlement to damages – breaches which entitle the innocent party to terminate the contract – conditions, warranties and innominate terms – damages and remoteness of damage.

Suggested Solution

A party to a contract is required to perform all the obligations which rest upon him. Breach of any obligation entitles the innocent party to a claim in damages. But some obligations are regarded as going to the root of the contract, and breach of such obligation entitles the innocent party, in addition to a claim for damages, to treat the breach as a repudiation of the contract, and to be able to bring the contract to an end.
   Whether the breach entitles the innocent party to terminate the contract depends on the nature of the term that has been breached. Traditionally terms were divided into conditions and warranties. A condition being a term which went to the root of the contract, the breach of which entitled the innocent party to terminate. A warranty is usefully defined in s61 Sale of Goods Act 1979 as being 'collateral to the main purpose of [the] contract, the breach of which gives rise to a claim for damages, but not to a right to reject the goods and treat the contract as repudiated.'
   There is a third category – innominate terms – of which further discussion will follow.
   It is not always easy to distinguish between a condition and a warranty; the distinction is often a fine one. Thus, in *Poussard* v *Spiers & Pond* (1) the failure of a performer to attend

for the opening performance was treated as a breach of condition, whereas the failure of a performer to attend on due date for rehearsals was treated as a breach of warranty *Bettini* v *Gye* (2). But, of course, the former breach might have had more serious consequences.

Certain criteria can be employed to determine whether a term is a condition. A term will be a condition in the following circumstances:

1. Where statute provides that it is a condition: see, for example, ss12–15 Sale of Goods Act 1979; ss8–11 Supply of Goods (Implied Terms) Act 1973; ss2–5 and 7–10 Supply of Goods and Services Act 1982.
2. Where binding authority requires a court to hold that it is a condition. Thus, in commercial contracts time is usually regarded as a condition: *The Mihalis Angelos* (3); *Bunge Corporation, New York* v *Tradax Export SA, Panama* (4). Where time is a condition any breach thereof is deemed to be repudiatory: *Union Eagle Ltd* v *Golden Achievement Ltd* (5).
3. Where the parties have agreed that it is a condition. But determining the intention of the parties is not without difficulty: see *L Schuler AG* v *Wickman Machine Tool Sales Ltd* (6) and compare *Lombard North Central plc* v *Butterworth* (7).

As noted above, where a term is a condition any breach of it will be deemed to be repudiatory; no regard will be had to the seriousness or consequences of the breach. But the courts have recognised that certain terms cannot readily be categorised as conditions or warranties. In *Hongkong Fir Shipping Co Ltd* v *Kawasaki Kisen Kaisha Ltd* (8) Diplock LJ said:

'Of such (terms) all that can be predicted is that some breaches will and others will not give rise to an event which will deprive the party not in default of substantially the whole benefit which it was intended that he should have obtained from the contract.'

These terms are called 'innominate terms', the third category referred to previously. This adds to the complexity of the classification. In *Bunge Corporation* v *Tradax* (above) Lord Scarman said that:

'Unless the contract makes it clear (either expressly or impliedly) that a particular stipulation is a condition or only a warranty, it is an innominate term the remedy for a breach of which depends on the nature, consequences and effect of the breach.'

This does add to the difficulty of determining when an innocent party can bring a contract to an end for breach.

With regard to damages, some attention has been paid to the question of remoteness of damage in the answer to Question 4, to which reference is invited. Some attention must, however, be given to other difficulties that may arise in the quantification of damages.

It has been said that the purpose of an award of damages for breach of contract is to put the injured party in the position he would have been in if his rights had been observed: *Robinson* v *Harman* (9); *Victoria Laundry (Windsor) Ltd* v *Newman Industries Ltd* (10). But Lord Hoffmann observed in *South Australia Asset Management Corp* v *York Montague Ltd* (11) that this is not always the correct point from which to start. At times giving effect to this purpose would be wholly disproportionate to the loss that had been sustained: see *Ruxley Electronics and Construction Ltd* v *Forsyth* (12).

There are further difficulties. In *Victoria Laundry* Asquith LJ said that the loss which could be recovered was that which was 'reasonably foreseeable'. In *The Heron II* (13) the House of Lords preferred the test to be 'in the reasonable contemplation of the parties' as denoting a higher degree of probability. Thus the loss suffered by the miller in having to close his mill in *Hadley v Baxendale* (14) was reasonably foreseeable, but not within the reasonable contemplation of the parties.

References

(1)   (1876) 1 QBD 410
(2)   (1876) 1 QBD 183
(3)   [1971] 1 QB 164
(4)   [1981] 2 All ER 513
(5)   [1997] 2 All ER 215
(6)   [1974] AC 235
(7)   [1987] 1 All ER 267
(8)   [1962] 2 QB 26
(9)   (1848) 1 Ex 850
(10)   [1949] 2 KB 528
(11)   [1996] 3 All ER 365
(12)   [1995] 3 All ER 268
(13)   [1969] 1 AC 350
(14)   (1854) 9 Exch 341

Examination Paper

University of London

LLB Examination June 2001

Elements of the Law of Contract

Zone A Examination Paper

Time allowed: **three** hours.
Answer **four** of the following **eight** questions.

1. On Monday, A posted a letter to B offering to buy B's vortex car for £12,000. The postman dropped the letter in the street where it was found by B's neighbour, C. He did not give the letter to B until Friday. In the meantime, on Tuesday, B wrote to A offering to sell the car to him for £11,000 and this letter arrived at A's house on Wednesday. A faxed to B stating, 'Good news! I agree to the deal.' However, because there was a paper failure in B's machine the message was never printed out. On Friday, B posted a letter to A agreeing to sell the car for £12,000. B's letter was not received by A for two weeks.

    Advise the parties. What difference, if any, would it make to your advice if the fax had been printed but B did not go into the room where the fax machine was situated for three days?

2. 'The present legal rules allowing an innocent party to bring a contract to an end for breach are unclear and in need for reform. Fortunately, the rules concerning measure of damages for breach are unclear.'

    Discuss.

3. D was an antique dealer who specialised in selling china. E went to D's shop and agreed to buy a teapot for £400. It was described by D as a 'Peppermint' pattern piece. E, who was a specialist teapot collector, knew that such a teapot was worth at least £600 but said nothing to D about the fact that he had underpriced the piece. The written agreement of sale which was signed by D and E contained an exemption clause limiting D's liability to a maximum of £100 for all breaches of contract. Three months later the teapot was certified by an expert auctioneer to be a 'Buckle' teapot and worth only £50.

    Advise E. What difference, if any, would it make to your advice if D had made no statement that it was a Peppermint piece but E believed it was Peppermint when he agreed to buy it?

4. Fanny, aged 17 years, agreed with Gertrude and Hildergard to form a pop group called 'The Glands'. They each agreed to pay £2,000 into a fund to buy a set of musical instruments and to split any profits equally between them. They bought the instruments, rehearsed and advertised their availability to perform at country house concerts.

a) Ian engaged The Glands to perform at a concert in his stately home but because of a nearby outbreak of foot and mouth disease the concert was called off by Ian a day before the concert was scheduled to take place. Ian required the £5,000 which he had paid in advanced to be returned. This the group refused to do.

b) Ken engaged The Glands to perform at his country house and agreed to pay the group £6,000. Their performance at the concert was so bad that many of the paying customers who were forced to listen to them began to slow hand clap before becoming restive and, in some cases, disruptive. Ken ordered the group off the stage to protect his property. He refused to pay The Glands anything relying on what he described as the poor quality of their performance.

c) Janice engaged The Glands to perform for £4,000 at her stately home and sold £25,000 worth of tickets. On the morning of the concert Hildergard gave premature birth to twins and, therefore, was unable to perform at the concert. Fanny and Gertrude refused to perform unless Janice paid an extra £5,000 for them to 'go on'. Because of the danger of damage to her property from angry fans Janice agreed to pay the additional sum. After the concert she paid Gertrude £4,000 and refused to pay the additional £5,000.

Advise Ian, Ken and Janice of their contractual liability.

5. Peter was a licensed dealer in pet food under the (fictional) Licensing of Pet Food Act 2001. Section 1 of the Act requires any person selling pet food to be licensed and if 'anyone shall trade in pet food without the appropriate licence he shall be guilty of a criminal offence.' Section 2 requires sales of pet food to be accompanied by a 'statutory invoice' which must contain details of the food supplied and a statement of the quantity supplied.

a) Peter supplied Queenie with pet food costing £500 but failed to provide a statutory invoice at the time of delivery because it had fallen out of the box in which it had been placed by Peter's employee. Queenie refused to pay for the pet food.

b) Peter supplied Robert with pet food but failed to provide a statutory invoice after Robert had said, 'Between friends no formalities are required.' Robert refused to pay for the pet food and claimed damages from Peter because, he claimed, the pet food was of poor quality.

c) Peter was paid £600 by Stephan for pet food to be delivered to Stephan's restaurant. Peter suspected that Stephan might be using the food for human consumption (which was prohibited by statute). It was subsequently, discovered that Stephan was using the pet food for this purpose. Stephan sought the repayment of the £600.

d) Peter agreed to supply pet food costing £2,000 to Thomas which Thomas paid for in advance. It was then discovered that, unknown to Peter, his licence had expired. Peter refused to deliver the pet food to Thomas or to return the £2,000 which Thomas had paid in advance.

Advise the parties.

6. 'The doctrine of privity has become largely irrelevant as a result of recent changes.' Discuss.

7. 'The present position where a party is mistaken about the identity of another contracting party is unsatisfactory.'
   Discuss.

8. Les agreed to rent his lorry to Morgan for £500 per week for 104 weeks. Morgan had just started out 'on his own' and was aiming to use the lorry to transport coal to a nearby power station. After paying the agreed sum for 14 weeks Morgan fell ill and Les agreed to accept £200 per week till Morgan recovered. Morgan paid the reduced sum for the following eight weeks when Morgan's wife, Noreen, won £250,000 on her premium savings bond. Although they had agreed to share any winnings Noreen refused to share any of her prize with Morgan. Ten weeks after Noreen's win, Morgan was left £10,000 by his Uncle Oliver. Morgan continued to pay the reduced sum till in the 52nd week Les discovered what had transpired. Two weeks later Morgan made a full recovery. Les claimed the full arrears of £300 per week and requested that the lorry be returned to Les immediately. Morgan refused. At that time Les could have rented the lorry for £600 per week.
   Advise Les.

Suggested Solutions

Question One

On Monday, A posted a letter to B offering to buy B's vortex car for £12,000. The postman dropped the letter in the street where it was found by B's neighbour, C. He did not give the letter to B until Friday. In the meantime, on Tuesday, B wrote to A offering to sell the car to him for £11,000 and this letter arrived at A's house on Wednesday. A faxed to B stating, 'Good news! I agree to the deal.' However, because there was a paper failure in B's machine the message was never printed out. On Friday, B posted a letter to A agreeing to sell the car for £12,000. B's letter was not received by A for two weeks.

Advise the parties. What difference, if any, would it make to your advice if the fax had been printed but B did not go into the room where the fax machine was situated for three days?

Suggested Solution

General Comment

This question on offer and acceptance invites discussion of the problems associated with instantaneous communication and the postal rule.

Skeleton Solution

A's offer, when it was communicated – B's offer and when it was communicated – A's fax message, whether it could be deemed to have been communicated – the position arising from B's failure to go to the room where the fax machine was situated – B's letter to A, was it communicated? – the application of the postal rule.

Suggested Solution

A has clearly made an offer to B to buy the car at the price of £12,000, and this offer is only communicated to B when the letter is handed to him on the Friday.

B's offer to sell to sell the car for £11,000 is communicated on the Wednesday. A's fax message in reply does appear to be an acceptance of that offer. The question is whether that acceptance has been communicated.

There is no direct authority on the communication of fax messages. In *Brinkibon* v *Stahag Stahl* (1) the House of Lords held that a telex message is communicated only when it is received, and it appears from *Entores Limited* v *Miles Far East Corporation* (2) that in instantaneous communications, such as the telephone, the acceptance is only communicated when it is actually heard. A's faxed acceptance, therefore, must have been received in order to have been validly communicated. The problem is the paper failure in B's machine.

B has not seen A's message of acceptance. We are not informed as to whether or not A is aware of this. If he is, then he knows that there has been no communication, and no contract has been concluded: this is the implication of Denning LJ's analysis of telex messages in *Entores* (above). If he is unaware of the failure, then can the acceptance be deemed to have been received by B?

If the paper failure can be attributed to fault on the part of B then, again following the reasoning of Denning LJ in the case just cited, B would be bound because, as his Lordship said, 'he would be estopped from saying that he did not receive the message.': this statement by Denning LJ was in the context of telephone conversations, but it is submitted that they apply also to fax messages. If B is not at fault, we must again refer to the remarks of Denning LJ, where he said 'But if there should be a case where the offeror without any fault on his part does not receive the message of acceptance – yet the sender of it reasonably believes that it has got home when it has not – then I think that there is no contract.'

It is convenient at this point to deal with the hypothesis that the fax had been printed but B did not go the room where the machine was situated for three days. In *The Brimnes* (3) the Court of Appeal held that a telex message could be deemed to have been received when it should have been read in the normal course of business. Note that this case concerned the termination of a contract, not its formation, but if its principle is applicable then B would be deemed to have received A's faxed acceptance when he should have read it, and a contract would have been concluded for the sale of the car at £11,000.

On the assumption that no contract has been concluded at that price I must consider the effect of B's letter to A.

On the Friday B posted a letter to A accepting the offer (which he had received that day) to buy the car for £12,000. This letter was not received for two weeks. This involves consideration of the postal rule.

In *Adams* v *Lindsell* (4) it was held that where the acceptance is sent by letter it is deemed to have been communicated when the letter was posted. The question is whether the postal rule applies in the present circumstances.

In *Henthorn* v *Fraser* (5) Lord Herschell said:

> '... where the circumstances are such that it must have been within the contemplation of the parties that, according to ordinary usages of mankind, the post might be used as a means of communicating the acceptance of an offer, the acceptance is complete as soon as it is posted.'

The use of the post was clearly within the contemplation of the parties: A's offer was by post, and B elected to use the post to communicate his acceptance.

How is the postal rule vitiated by the delay in the receipt of the letter? In *Household Fire Insurance Co* v *Grant* (6) Thesiger LJ held that the application of the postal rule meant that contract was made as soon as the letter was posted. It could not, therefore, be 'unmade' by a vagary in the post.

It appears, therefore, that a contract was concluded by the exchange of letters for the sale of the car at £12,000.

A would obviously prefer to be able to enforce the sale at £11,000, but would only be able to do so if he could establish fault on B's part, either because of the paper failure in the fax machine or because of B's failure to go to room where it was situated.

References

(1)   [1983] 2 AC 34
(2)   [1955] 2 QB 327
(3)   [1975] QB 929
(4)   (1818) B & Ald 681
(5)   [1892] 2 Ch 27
(6)   (1879) 4 Ex D 216

Question Two

'The present legal rules allowing an innocent party to bring a contract to an end for breach are unclear and in need for reform. Fortunately, the rules concerning measure of damages for breach are unclear.'

Discuss.

Suggested Solution

General Comment

This question is very similar to the one set in the examination for the year 2000, but a different emphasis seems to be required. The focus should be on the difficulties in treating a breach of contract as repudiatory, especially with regard to innominate terms. This should be contrasted with the suggested clarity concerning the measure of damages.

Skeleton Solution

The relative importance of terms: conditions, warranties and innominate terms – the criteria for establishing that a term is a condition – the category of innominate terms and the difficulties this creates – the rules concerning the measure of damages.

Suggested Solution

An innocent party is only entitled to bring a contract to an end for breach if that breach is of a condition or is treated as such. For a breach of warranty the innocent party's remedy is only for damages. A term is a condition if statute so provides, or there is binding authority requiring such interpretation, or if such was the parties' intention.

Certain terms are classified as conditions by statute: inter alia, by ss12–15 Sale of Goods Act 1979. The strict application of the statute has been the subject of criticism following the case of *Arcos Ltd v E A Ronaasen & Son* (1) where the breach was of s13 Sale of Goods Act 1979 (sale by description) but the breach was slight, and was seized on by the buyer in order to take advantage of a falling market. (This would now fall within s15A of the Act, whereby a slight breach could be treated as only a breach of warranty.) In *Cehave NV v Bremer Handelsgesellschaft mbH, The Hansa Nord* (2) the breach was of the term 'shipped in good condition', but the Court of Appeal refused to treat this as a breach of the 'merchantable quality' condition in the Sale of Goods Act 1979 (as the section then read) as its consequences did not justify termination of the contract.

Binding authority requires certain terms to be treated as conditions, for example stipulations as to time in commercial contracts: *The Mihalis Angelos* (3); *Bunge Corporation, New York* v *Tradax Export SA, Panama* (4).

Where the classification of the term as a condition reflects the intention of the parties, the courts will so treat it – subject to a situation such as that in *L Schuler AG* v *Wickman Machine Tools Sales Ltd* (5). The consequences of so doing can be harsh, even unjust: see *Lombard North Central plc* v *Butterworth* (6).

The major difficulties that arise, however, stem from the category of the innominate term.

The origin of the development of the innominate term is in the judgment of Diplock LJ in *Hongkong Fir Shipping Co Ltd* v *Kawasaki Kisen Kaisha Ltd* (7) where he said:

> 'There are many … contractual undertakings … which cannot be categorised as being "conditions" or "warranties" … Of such undertakings all that can be predicted is that some breaches will and others will not give rise to an event which will deprive the party not in default of substantially the whole benefit which it was intended that he should obtain.'

In *Bunge Corporation* v *Tradax* (above) Lord Scarman said;

> 'Unless the contract makes it clear … that a particular stipulation is a condition or only a warranty, it is an innominate term the remedy for a breach of which depends on the nature, consequences and effect of the breach.'

This leads to uncertainty; the consequences of the breach have to be awaited before the relevant term can be classified, which means that the parties cannot be sure of their obligations at the time they concluded the contract. This has also created problems for the Courts. For example, in *The Naxos* (8) the majority of the House of Lords held that the obligation of the seller to have the cargo ready for delivery at a particular time was a condition, whereas the majority of the Court of Appeal and the judge at first instance held that it was not.

In the context of anticipatory breach it has occurred that a breach, on the face of it comparatively trivial, was treated as repudiatory because of the consequences that ensued: *Federal Commerce & Navigation Co Ltd* v *Molena Alpha Inc* (9).

Whilst there is the need for certainty, too much emphasis on it can lead to injustice as in the case of *Arcos* v *Ronaasen* (above). The courts have on occasions been reluctant to treat a breach as a breach of condition, particularly where an award of damages would prove an adequate remedy. It remains to consider the rules concerning the measure of damages.

The purpose of an award of damages is to put the innocent party in the position he would have been in if the contract had been performed: *Robinson* v *Harman* (10); *Victoria Laundry (Windsor) Ltd* v *Newman Industries Ltd* (11). But, as Asquith LJ observed in the latter case:

> 'This purpose, if relentlessly pursued, would provide him with a complete indemnity for all loss *de facto* resulting from a particular breach, however improbable, however unpredictable. This, in contract at least, is recognised as too harsh a rule.'

The important limitation on the implementation of this purpose is that the damages must not be too remote. The rule is that the damages:

'... should be such as may be fairly and reasonably be considered either arising naturally, that is, according to the usual course of things, from the breach of contract itself, or such as may be reasonably be supposed to have been in the contemplation of both parties at the time they made the contract as the probable result of the breach of it': *Hadley* v *Baxendale* (12) per Alderson B.

Some ambiguity has resulted from this rule. In *Victoria Laundry* Asquith LJ defined the test as 'reasonable foreseeability', but the House of Lords in *The Heron II* (13) preferred the test to be formulated as 'within the reasonable contemplation of the parties', which denoted a higher degree of probability.

It should be noted that if the party in default should have foreseen (or contemplated) the type of damage that would probably have resulted from the breach, it will not avail him that the extent of such damage could not have been within reasonable contemplation: *H Parsons (Livestock) Ltd* v *Uttley Ingham & Co Ltd* (14).

References

(1)   [1933] AC 470
(2)   [1976] QB 44
(3)   [1971] 1 QB 164
(4)   [1981] 2 All ER 513
(5)   [1974] AC 235
(6)   [1987] 1 All ER 267
(7)   [1962[2 QB 26
(8)   [1990] 1 WLR 1337
(9)   [1979] AC 757
(10)   (1848) 1 Ex 850
(11)   [1949] 2 KB 528
(12)   (1854) 9 Exch 341
(13)   [1969] 1 AC 350
(14)   [1978] 1 All ER 525

Question Three

D was an antique dealer who specialised in selling china. E went to D's shop and agreed to buy a teapot for £400. It was described by D as a 'Peppermint' pattern piece. E, who was a specialist teapot collector, knew that such a teapot was worth at least £600 but said nothing to D about the fact that he had underpriced the piece. The written agreement of sale which was signed by D and E contained an exemption clause limiting D's liability to a maximum of £100 for all breaches of contract. Three months later the teapot was certified by an expert auctioneer to be a 'Buckle' teapot and worth only £50.

Advise E. What difference, if any, would it make to your advice if D had made no statement that it was a Peppermint piece but E believed it was Peppermint when he agreed to buy it?

Suggested Solution

General Comment

A number of issues are raised by this question: the possible sale by description; misrepresentation; common mistake and unilateral mistake; and the effect of the exemption clause.

Skeleton Solution

Whether the description invokes s13 Sale of Goods Act 1979 – whether there has been an actionable misrepresentation – whether the contract is void at law for common mistake, and if not the possible remedy in equity – the variation of the question suggesting unilateral mistake – the effect of the exemption clause.

Suggested Solution

The teapot was described as a "Peppermint". Under s13(1) Sale of Goods Act 1979 there is the implied term that the goods correspond with the description. But in *Harlingdon & Leinster Enterprises Ltd* v *Christopher Hull Fine Art Ltd* (1) Nourse LJ said that 'The description must have a sufficient influence in the sale to become an essential term of the contract and the correlative of influence is reliance.' E could not be held to have reasonably relied on the description, as he was a specialist in the area and knew that such a teapot was worth considerably more than the price he paid. It would appear that E cannot invoke the statute, but I have some reservations about this view, as the facts here are not quite on all fours with those in the case cited, where the seller expressly disclaimed knowledge of the paintings in question.

It also seems doubtful whether E could successfully found a claim based on misrepresentation. Whilst the description of the teapot does constitute a representation, the difficulty would be in establishing that it induced him to enter into the contract for the reasons set out above.

On the assumption that both parties shared the mistaken belief that the teapot was a 'Peppermint', I must examine the effect of this common mistake, which is as to the quality of the subject matter.

At common law, where mistake is operative, the effect is to render the contract void. Operative common mistake at common law has been confined to very narrow limits by the decision of the House of Lords in *Bell* v *Lever Brothers Ltd* (2). In his speech in that case, Lord Atkin held:

> '… a mistake will not affect assent unless it is the mistake of both parties, and is as to existence of some quality which makes the thing without the quality essentially different from the thing as it was believed to be.'

Lord Atkin would have applied this test somewhat restrictively. One of the examples his Lordship gave of a mistake that would not be operative is the sale of a picture which both parties believe to be the work of an old master and turns out to be a modern copy.

The speeches and decision in *Bell* v *Lever Bros* were analysed by Steyn J in *Associated Japanese Bank International Ltd* v *Credit du Nord SA* (3), where the learned judge rejected the view that had been advanced by some commentators that the decision of the House of Lords made it virtually impossible to find a mistake as to quality which would render the contract void. His Lordship conceded that this would be rare, but he would have found that such mistake had this effect on the facts before him, but he decided the case on other grounds.

Whilst it is theoretically possible for a mistake as to quality to render the contract void, it is difficult to find a satisfactory case where this has been so. I must conclude that the present contract would not be void at common law. (In *Associated Japanese Bank* Steyn J advanced the proposition that a person could not rely on a mistake where he had no reasonable grounds for the belief: he referred to *McRae* v *Commonwealth Disposals Commission* (4). This may be relevant here, considering E's knowledge and expertise.)

The next question is whether equitable relief would be available to E. In *Solle* v *Butcher* (5) the Court of Appeal held that a contract although not void at law, was susceptible to being voidable in equity. Denning LJ held:

> 'A contract is also liable in equity to be set aside if the parties were under a common misapprehension either as to facts or as to their relative and respective rights, provided that the misapprehension was fundamental and that the party seeking to set it aside was not himself at fault.'*

Some uncertainty attaches to this equitable principle. *Solle* v *Butcher* was followed in *Grist* v *Bailey* (6) and in *Laurence* v *Lexcourt Holdings Ltd* (7), but the correctness of these two decisions was doubted by Hoffmann LJ in *William Sindall plc* v *Cambridgeshire County Council* (8). Moreover, it is doubtful whether equity would come to E's assistance, given that he was quite prepared to take advantage of D's considerable underpricing.

I must submit, therefore, that the contract is neither void nor voidable.

I propose at this point to deal with the variation of the facts introduced in the last paragraph of the question. Here the mistake is unilateral. It is, I submit, clear on the authority of *Smith* v *Hughes* (9) that this would not, in law, invalidate the contract. Nor would rescission in equity be available for the unilateral mistake: *Riverlate Properties Ltd* v *Paul* (10).

E cannot, therefore rely on mistake. If I am correct that there has been no breach of sale by description, and no actionable misrepresentation, E has no remedy, and the exemption clause is irrelevant. But as I have conceded the possibility of there being either a breach of contract or a misrepresentation, I must consider the exemption clause in the light of those possibilities.

If there had been an actionable misrepresentation, the exemption clause would not apply, as it referred only to breaches of contract. The right of rescission would appear to be barred by the three months' delay. There is nothing to suggest fraud on D's part, but E would be entitled to damages under s2(1) Misrepresentation Act 1967. It is unlikely that D could discharge the onus imposed on him by the statute. The measure of damages, in tort, would be the difference between the price E paid for the teapot and its actual worth.

What would the effect of the clause have been if there had been a breach of contract? The clause had clearly been incorporated in the contract by E's signature thereto: *L'Estrange* v *F Graucob Ltd* (11). But as the breach would have been of s13 Sale of Goods Act 1979, the clause would have been subject to the Unfair Contract Terms Act 1977. It can be assumed that E was dealing as a consumer, and s6(2) of that Act would render the clause totally ineffective. The clause would also fall foul of the Unfair Terms in Consumer Contracts Regulations 1999. E would have lost his right to reject, again because of the delay of three months, but would be entitled to damages, The measure being the difference between the actual value of the teapot – £50 – and the value it would have had if it had corresponded with the description – apparently at least £600: s53(3) Sale of Goods Act 1979.

Note: This appears to be no longer correct. In the Court of Appeal in *Great Peace Shipping Limited* v *Tsavliris (International) Limited* in a judgment dated 14 October 2002 ((2002) The Times 17 October) Lord Phillips MR, delivering the judgment of the Court, said:

> 'In this case we have heard full argument, which has provided what we believe has been the first opportunity in this court for a full and mature consideration of the relation between *Bell* v *Lever Brothers Limited* and *Solle* v *Butcher*. In the light of that consideration we can see no way that *Solle* v *Butcher* can stand with *Bell* v *Lever Brothers Limited*. In these circumstances we can see no option but so to hold.'

References

(1)   [1990] 3 WLR 13
(2)   [1932] AC 161
(3)   [1988] 3 All ER 902
(4)   (1951) 84 CLR 377
(5)   [1950] 1 KB 671
(6)   [1967] Ch 532
(7)   [1978] 1 WLR 1128

References (contd.)

(8)   [1994] 3 All ER 932
(9)   (1871) LR 6 QB 597
(10)   [1975] Ch 133
(11)   [1934] 2 KB 394

Question Four

Fanny, aged 17 years, agreed with Gertrude and Hildergard to form a pop group called 'The Glands'. They each agreed to pay £2,000 into a fund to buy a set of musical instruments and to split any profits equally between them. They bought the instruments, rehearsed and advertised their availability to perform at country house concerts.

a) Ian engaged The Glands to perform at a concert in his stately home but because of a nearby outbreak of foot and mouth disease the concert was called off by Ian a day before the concert was scheduled to take place. Ian required the £5,000 which he had paid in advanced to be returned. This the group refused to do.

b) Ken engaged The Glands to perform at his country house and agreed to pay the group £6,000. Their performance at the concert was so bad that many of the paying customers who were forced to listen to them began to slow hand clap before becoming restive and, in some cases, disruptive. Ken ordered the group off the stage to protect his property. He refused to pay The Glands anything relying on what he described as the poor quality of their performance.

c) Janice engaged The Glands to perform for £4,000 at her stately home and sold £25,000 worth of tickets. On the morning of the concert Hildergard gave premature birth to twins and, therefore, was unable to perform at the concert. Fanny and Gertrude refused to perform unless Janice paid an extra £5,000 for them to 'go on'. Because of the danger of damage to her property from angry fans Janice agreed to pay the additional sum. After the concert she paid Gertrude £4,000 and refused to pay the additional £5,000.

Advise Ian, Ken and Janice of their contractual liability.

Suggested Solution

General Comment

The main topic to be discussed here is the doctrine of frustration. Attention will also have to be paid to the possible breach of contract in one of the situations, and to the question of duress in another.

Skeleton Solution

The situation postulated in (a): when frustration of a contract occurs, and the limitations of the doctrine; the effect of the doctrine at common law and the application of the Law Reform (Frustrated Contracts) Act 1943 – the situation in (b): whether there has been frustration or a breach of contract – the situation in (c): whether the contract has been frustrated; the issue of duress.

Suggested Solution

Situation (a)

In *Davis Contractors Ltd* v *Fareham Urban District Council* (1) Lord Radcliffe held that:

> ' ... frustration occurs whenever the law recognises that without default of either party a contractual obligation has become incapable of being performed because the circumstances in which performance is called for would render it a thing radically different from that which was undertaken by the contract.'

The effect of frustration is to discharge the parties from further obligations: *Taylor* v *Caldwell* (2).

But there are limits to the operation of the doctrine. The mere fact that the contract takes longer to perform than was envisaged, or proves more expensive, or more difficult, is not in itself sufficient to constitute frustration: see *Davis Contractors* (above); *British Movietone News Ltd* v *London & District Cinemas Ltd* (3); *The Eugenia* (4); *The Nema* (5).

Ian cancels the contract because of the outbreak of foot and mouth disease. It is not possible on this limited information to determine with certainty whether this outbreak constitutes a frustrating event, but for the sake of further exposition I shall assume that it does.

The parties are, therefore, discharged from further obligations. The Glands have incurred certain expenses and Ian has made an advance payment. In order to see how the rights of the parties would be adjusted with regard to the expenses and the advance payment we must turn to the Law Reform (Frustrated Contracts) Act 1943.

Section 1(2) provides that advance payments are recoverable, subject to the proviso that if the party to whom it was made had incurred expenses in the performance of the contract the court has a discretion to allow him to retain, from the advance payment, an amount not exceeding such expenses. In *Gamerco SA* v *ICM/Fair Warning (Agency) Ltd* (6) Garland J held that the court has a broad discretion in this regard; it may allow the retention of all, or some, or none of those expenses. The expenses incurred by The Glands have not been quantified, and it appears that they might have been incurred before the conclusion of this particular contract; nor do we know what loss Ian has sustained by the cancellation of the concert. It may well be that the court would allow Ian to recover the advance payment, without deduction, as it did in the case just cited. (No valuable benefit has been conferred, so s1(3) does not apply.)

Situation (b)

The doctrine of frustration does not appear to apply in this situation, unless one could regard the behaviour of the audience as a frustrating event. But this was occasioned by the 'so bad' performance of The Glands. The frustration might be said to be self-induced; negligence can constitute self-inducement: *J Lauritzen AS* v *Wijsmuller BV, The 'Super Servant Two'* (7). Lord Radcliffe in *Davis Contractors* (above) emphasised that the circumstances must have arisen 'without default of either party'.

The Glands appear to have been in breach of the implied term that they would perform their services with reasonable care and skill: s13 Supply of Goods and Services Act 1982. The consequences of the breach would seem to have justified Ken in terminating the contract. If they did not, he would have been in breach.

Situation (c)
I do not think that the frustration (if there was one) could be regarded as self-induced. Self-inducement must consist of a deliberate act, as in *Maritime National Fish Ltd v Ocean Trawlers Ltd* (8); or negligence (above).

The question is, however, whether Hildegard's inability to perform can constitute frustration. Incapacity of one of the parties can be a frustrating event: *Condor v The Barron Knights Ltd* (9). But there only one performer was involved. The concert could have been performed by the two other members of the group, albeit in a different manner from the one intended.

The refusal by Fanny and Gertrude to perform unless Janice paid the additional sum amounts to a threat to break a contract. This constitutes duress. This can be defined as illegitimate pressure, which gives the victim no choice but to submit: *Universe Tankships Inc of Monrovia v International Transport Workers' Federation* (10). This appears to be applicable here. This form of economic duress has been recognised in a number of cases: for example, *B & S Contracts and Design Ltd v Victor Green Publications Ltd* (11); *Atlas Express Ltd v Kafco Ltd* (12). Janice would, therefore, be justified in refusing to pay the additional £5,000.

In any event no fresh consideration has been furnished for the promise to pay this additional amount: *Stilk v Myrick* (13). *Williams v Roffey Bros and Nicholls (Contractors) Ltd* (14) would not apply because of the presence of duress.

(It is somewhat difficult to comprehend what purpose is served by introducing the fact that Fanny is a minor in law. Suffice it to say that the contracts with Ian, Ken and Janice, being to her benefit as a whole, would be binding on her. Her agreement with the other two members of The Glands constitutes a partnership and would be voidable at her instance.)

References

(1)   [1956] AC 696
(2)   (1863) 3 B & S 826
(3)   [1952] AC 166
(4)   [1964] 2 QB 226
(5)   [1982] AC 724
(6)   [1995] 1 WLR 1226
(7)   [1990] 1 Lloyd's Rep 1
(8)   [1935] AC 324
(9)   [1966] 1 WLR 87
(10)   [1983] AC 366
(11)   [1984] ICR 419
(12)   [1989] QB 833
(13)   (1809) 2 Camp 317
(14)   [1990] 2 WLR 1153

Question Five

Peter was a licensed dealer in pet food under the (fictitional) Licensing of Pet Food Act 2001. Section 1 of the Act requires any person selling pet food to be licensed and if 'anyone shall trade in pet food without the appropriate licence he shall be guilty of a criminal offence.' Section 2 requires sales of pet food to be accompanied by a 'statutory invoice' which must contain details of the food supplied and a statement of the quantity supplied.

a) Peter supplied Queenie with pet food costing £500 but failed to provide a statutory invoice at the time of delivery because it had fallen out of the box in which it had been placed by Peter's employee. Queenie refused to pay for the pet food.

b) Peter supplied Robert with pet food but failed to provide a statutory invoice after Robert had said, 'Between friends no formalities are required.' Robert refused to pay for the pet food and claimed damages from Peter because, he claimed, the pet food was of poor quality.

c) Peter was paid £600 by Stephan for pet food to be delivered to Stephan's restaurant. Peter suspected that Stephan might be using the food for human consumption (which was prohibited by statute). It was subsequently, discovered that Stephan was using the pet food for this purpose. Stephan sought the repayment of the £600.

d) Peter agreed to supply pet food costing £2,000 to Thomas which Thomas paid for in advance. It was then discovered that, unknown to Peter, his licence had expired. Peter refused to deliver the pet food to Thomas or to return the £2,000 which Thomas had paid in advance.

Advise the parties.

Suggested Solution

General Comment

This area of the law, illegal contracts, has been a favoured topic for the examiners over the past few years. It requires exploration of whether the contract is illegal as formed, or merely illegal in its performance. In this context the effects of the illegal contract must be examined to determine whether it is enforceable by either party.

Skeleton Solution

The purpose of the Act, whether it totally prohibits the conclusion or performance of a contract, or merely penalises behaviour – the consequent position of the guilty and innocent parties, whether either can enforce the contract – the application of the principles derived to each of the situations presented – the possibility of restitutionary claims.

Suggested Solution

The general rule is as follows.

Where the statute (or regulation) totally prohibits a contract neither party can enforce it: *Re Mahmoud & Ispahani* (1). Where the statute merely prescribes a method of performance of the contract, coupled with a sanction for non-compliance, the innocent party may be able to enforce it, provided it is not against public policy to allow this: *Archbolds (Freightage) Ltd* v *S Spanglett Ltd* (2). On the latter interpretation of the statute, the guilty party may also be able to enforce the contract, provided again that this would not be against public policy: *St John's Shipping Corporation* v *Joseph Rank Ltd* (3). This general statement of the law is supported by the judgment of Kerr LJ in *Phoenix General Insurance Co Greece SA* v *Administration Asigurarilor de Stat* (4).

It is now necessary to apply these principles to each of the contracts into which Peter entered.

a) *The contract with Queenie*

Peter's failure to deliver the statutory invoice appears to have been inadvertent: he did not intend to perform the contract in an illegal manner. Despite this I incline to the view that Peter could not enforce the contract. In *Anderson Ltd* v *Daniel* (5) where the seller delivered goods without the required invoice stating the percentage of certain chemicals therein, he was denied enforcement: he had failed to perform the contract in the only way it was permitted. In *Marles* v *Philip Trant & Sons Ltd* (6) Denning LJ approved this decision, and referring to the antecedent transaction in the case before him he said 'The seed merchants [the original sellers] performed [their contract] in an illegal way in that they omitted to furnish the prescribed particulars. That renders the contract unenforceable by them.' (It did not render a subsequent transaction illegal.)

It is possible that Peter could have a restitutionary claim, not for the purchase price but on a quantum valebat basis. In *Mohamed* v *Alaga & Co* (7) the Court of Appeal allowed a restitutionary claim for reasonable remuneration for services performed under an illegal contract on a quantum meruit basis. But whether that decision could be applied to this situation is uncertain. The restitutionary principle will not be invoked where it would be against public policy to do so: *Awwad* v *Geraghty & Co* (8). It is conceivable that it would be against public policy to apply the principle in the case of foodstuff.

b) *The contract with Robert*

Here both parties intended to perform the contract in an illegal manner. In *St John's Shipping Corporation* v *Joseph Rank Ltd* (above) Devlin J held:

> ' ... a contract which is entered into with the object of committing an illegal act is unenforceable. The application of this principle depends upon the proof of intent, at the time the contract was made, to break the law; if the intent is mutual the contract is not enforceable at all ...'

The intent to break the law in this instance was clearly mutual. This debars Peter from claiming the purchase price and Robert from seeking a remedy in damages. A further barrier to Robert's claim would be the decision in *Ashmore, Benson Pease & Co Ltd* v *A V Dawson Ltd* (9) (participation in the illegality).

c) *The contract with Stephan*

Stephan is purchasing the pet food for an illegal purpose. Peter is apparently aware of this. This knowledge would debar enforcement on his part; he would have participated in the illegality: *Ashmore Benson etc* (above).

Because of the illegal purpose the contract would also be unenforceable by Stephan. It is not clear from the question whether Stephan has in general used pet food for human consumption or if he has so used this particular consignment. If he has not yet used this particular consignment for that purpose he may be able to recover the £600 provided that he repudiates the illegal purpose before it has been implemented.

d) *The contract with Thomas*

As Peter has traded without the requisite licence the contract is illegal as formed and neither party can enforce it. If this is unknown to Thomas, he might, as an innocent party, be able to recover the £2,000 on a restitutionary basis.

References

(1)   [1921] 2 KB 716
(2)   [1961] 1 QB 174
(3)   [1957] 1 QB 267
(4)   [1987] 2 All ER 152
(5)   [1924] 1 KB 138
(6)   [1954] 1 QB 29
(7)   [1999] 3 All ER 699
(8)   [2000] 1 All ER 608
(9)   [1973] 2 All ER 856

Question Six

'The doctrine of privity has become largely irrelevant as a result of recent changes.'
   Discuss.

Suggested Solution

General Comment

What is required here is a discussion of the current status of the doctrine of privity of contract; an examination of the rules concerning the conferring of benefits; and the imposition of liabilities on third parties and the modifications to those rules effected by the Contracts (Rights of Third Parties) Act 1999.

Skeleton Solution

Privity of contract: the two rules; the conferring of benefits and the imposition of liabilities – the conferring of benefits; the common law rules and the modifications of those rules by the 1999 Act – the imposition of liabilities; the current law.

Suggested Solution

The doctrine of privity of contract involves the application of the two rules: one, that a person could not enforce a benefit conferred on him by a contract to which he was not a party; two, that a person cannot have a liability imposed on him by a contract to which he was not a party. I shall examine each of these rules in turn.

The conferring of a benefit
In *Dunlop Pneumatic Tyre Co Ltd* v *Selfridge & Co Ltd* (1) Viscount Haldane LC held as a fundamental principle in the law of England 'that only a person who is a party to a contract can sue on it.' This meant that even where a contract expressly conferred a benefit on a third party, he could not enforce it.

   The rule derives from the decision in *Tweddle* v *Atkinson* (2) and was reaffirmed by the House of Lords in *Beswick* v *Beswick* (3). In that case the promisor had contracted with his uncle to pay a pension to the uncle's widow on the former's death, and when he failed to do so the widow, not being a party to the contract, could not enforce the promise in her personal capacity.

   Whilst the promisee might be able to enforce the promise, he could not, as a rule, claim for the third party's loss: *Woodar Investment Development Ltd* v *Wimpey Construction Ltd* (4); *Forster* v *Silvermere Golf and Equestrian Centre* (5). The exceptional situation is where it is found that it was within the contemplation of the contracting parties that any breach of it would cause loss to an identifiable third party.

The rule had long been criticised. Attempts to circumvent it by the trust concept were largely unsuccessful: see *Re Schebsman* (6); *Vandepitte* v *Preferred Accident Corp of New York* (7).

Attempts to confer the benefit of an exemption clause on third parties created difficulties. The third party could not rely on the exemption clause in a contract in *Scruttons Ltd* v *Midland Silicones Ltd* (8). Allowing a third party to enforce an exemption clause was obtained in *The Eurymedon* (9) and *The New York Star* (10) by the somewhat questionable approach of inferring a contract between the promisor and the third party.

The rule as to conferring a benefit on a third party has not been abrogated, but has been substantially modified by the Contracts (Rights of Third Parties) Act 1999. The Act allows a third party to enforce a contract in specified circumstances. (*Note*: This dispenses with the usual requirement that consideration must move from the promisee.)

Section1(1) of the 1999 Act sets out the circumstances in which a third party can enforce a term of the contract: (a) where the contract expressly provides that he may; and (b) where the term purports to confer a benefit on him. But s1(1)(b) does not apply if it appears that the parties did not intend the term to be enforceable by the third party: s1(2).

Section 1(3) provides the important requirement that the third party must be expressly identified in the contract by name, class or description. But the third party need not be in existence when the contract is made. This allows the contracting parties to confer enforceable rights on, for example, an unborn child, a future spouse or a company that has not yet been incorporated.

It is open to the contracting parties to limit or place conditions on the third party's rights of enforcement (s1(4)); but subject to that the third party will have available to him the remedies for breach of contract that would have been available if he had been a contracting party: s1(5).

The question of third party enforcement of exemption clauses is dealt with in s1(6) which makes it clear that the Act enables a third party to take advantage of an exemption clause in a contract.

It may be possible for the contracting parties to rescind or vary the contract subject to the provisions of s2.

This does not purport to be an exhaustive exposition of the Act, merely of its salient provisions. But it is clear from the above discussion that there will be situations where the Act does not apply.

When the Act does not apply certain difficulties may remain. Thus, in *Panatown Ltd* v *Alfred McAlpine Construction Ltd* (11) the claimant contracted with the defendant to do building work on land owned by a third party and required the defendant to execute a deed giving the latter a remedy for any failure to exercise reasonable care and skill. Alleging breach of contract, the claimant, who had not suffered any loss, sought damages for the loss suffered by the third party. The House of Lords held by a majority that the claim could not succeed. The exception to the rule regarding recovery for a third party's loss (mentioned above) did not apply where it was intended that the third party should have a direct claim against the defendant.

Imposing a liability

The common law rule in this regard is unaffected by the Act. It remains the position that a person cannot have a liability imposed on him by a contract to which he was not a party. The one real exception to this is in the law of property where restrictive covenants relating to the use of land may bind successors in title to the land: *Tulk* v *Moxhay* (12).

Whilst a person cannot have contractual liability imposed on him by a contract to which he was a stranger, he may incur liability in tort if he induces a breach of that contract or interferes with the contractual rights of the contracting parties: *Lumley* v *Gye* (13); *British Motor Trade Association* v *Salvadori* (14); *Law Debenture Trust Corporation* v *Ural Caspian Oil Corporation* (15).

It is thus incorrect to state that the doctrine of privity 'has become largely irrelevant'. The common law rules will still obtain with regard the the conferring of benefits where the 1999 Act does not apply and remain in force with regard to the imposition of liabilities.

References

(1)   [1915] AC 847
(2)   (1861) 1 B & S 393
(3)   [1968] AC 58
(4)   [1980] 1 WLR 277
(5)   (1981) 125 SJ 397
(6)   [1944] Ch 83
(7)   [1933] AC 70
(8)   [1962] AC 446
(9)   [1975[AC 154
(10)   [1981] 1 WLR 138
(11)   [2000] 4 All ER 97
(12)   (1848) 2 Ph 774
(13)   (1853) 2 E & B 216
(14)   [1949] Ch 556
(15)   [1993] 2 All ER 355

Question Seven

'The present position where a party is mistaken about the identity of another contracting party is unsatisfactory.'

Discuss.

Suggested Solution

General Comment

This should not have been a difficult question to answer: there are well established cases. But a mere recital of the case law would not have been sufficient. For a good answer an analysis of the problem should have been attempted.

Skeleton Solution

The nature of the problem – void and voidable contracts and the consequences of this classification – the situation where the parties are negotiating at a distance, and where they are face to face – the difficulties in distinguishing some of the cases from each other – the solution to the problem?

Suggested Solution

Where one party is mistaken as to the identity of the other contracting party, this mistake can render the contract void, or merely voidable. In virtually all the cases we shall be considering, the contract involved the sale of goods by their original owner to a person who had misrepresented his identity and the latter's subsequent disposal of those goods to a third party. The courts are then faced with the task of deciding which of two innocent parties should bear the loss.

If the contract is void, no rights can flow from it, property did not pass to the imposter, and the owner can recover the goods from whoever has them in his possession. If, however, the misrepresentation merely renders the contract voidable, the original owner's claim for recovery of the goods might be defeated by the operation of s23 Sale of Goods Act 1979. Under this section, where the imposter sells the goods to a third party, the seller (the imposter) has a voidable title to the goods, but if his title had not been avoided at the time of the sale, the third party buyer acquires good title to the goods provided that he bought them in good faith and without notice of the seller's defect of title.

An early and perhaps unusual case (incidentally not involving disposition to a third party) is that of *Boulton* v *Jones* (1). The defendant had a running account with a Mr Brocklehurst against whom he had a set-off. He addressed an order for goods to

58

Brocklehurst which he sent to the latter's place of business. Unknown to the defendant Brocklehurst had disposed of his business to the plaintiff who substituted his own name on the order and supplied the goods. The contract between the plaintiff and the defendant was held to be void. Whilst this was a justifiable application of the principle that an offer addressed to one party cannot be accepted by another, the case had curious consequences. The plaintiff, who was apparently unaware of the set-off, could not recover the purchase price, nor the goods as they had been consumed, and the defendant obtained the benefit of the goods without having to pay for them and still retained his rights against Brocklehurst. This represents one unsatisfactory aspect of the law involving mistake as to identity.

In *Cundy* v *Lindsay* (2) the rogue, when ordering goods, had sought to give the impression that he was the reputable firm Blenkiron & Co (known to the owner of the goods) by styling himself A Blenkarn and giving an address in the same street but at a different number from the reputable firm. The owners, believing that they were contracting with the firm they knew, dispatched the goods to the address given by the rogue, who then sold them to an innocent third party. The House of Lords held that the contract with the rogue was void for mistake. The owners' intention had been to contract with Blenkiron & Co, not with the author of the order at the address that had been given. In contrast in *King's Norton Metal Co Ltd* v *Edridge Merret & Co Ltd* (3) the rogue placed an order, describing himself as trading as Hallam & Co – which was fictitious. The Court of Appeal held that as Hallam & Co did not exist the intention could only have been to contract with the writer of the order: the contract was therefore voidable and not void. These two cases are not all that clearly distinguishable.

Further uncertainties emerge from a consideration of the cases in which the parties contracted inter praesentes, in each others' presence. In *Phillips* v *Brooks Ltd* (4) the rogue entered a jeweller's shop falsely announcing himself as a titled personage. This persuaded the shopkeeper to part with an item of jewellery for a worthless cheque. Before the fraud was discovered the rogue had sold the jewellery in question to an innocent third party who, by virtue of s23 Sale of Goods Act 1979, obtained good title. The jeweller's contract with the rogue had been merely voidable, not void.

On similar facts a contrary decision was reached in *Ingram* v *Little* (5). In purchasing a car, the rogue had proffered a cheque in payment, which the plaintiff found unacceptable and declared that 'the deal was off'. Thereupon, the rogue falsely declared that he was a Mr Hutchinson and furnished certain addresses. After checking these addresses the plaintiff was satisfied and allowed the rogue to take the car in return for the cheque. Here the rights of the innocent third party, to whom the car was subsequently sold, did not prevail. The contract between the plaintiff and the rogue had been void for mistake. Pearce LJ held that *Phillips* v *Brooks Ltd* was a borderline case, decided on its own facts. Devlin LJ dissented, holding that there was a presumption 'that a person is intending to contract with the person to whom he is actually addressing the words of contract'.

A case similar to the above two is *Lewis* v *Averay* (6), the facts of which are virtually indistinguishable from *Ingram* v *Little*. Here a cheque was accepted in payment for the purchase of a car after the rogue had produced a fraudulent document purporting to prove that he was Richard Greene (then a well known actor). The Court of Appeal held that this deceit rendered the contract voidable, and not void, and the innocent third party's rights prevailed. Lord Denning MR stated what he believed to be the true principle: his Lordship said:

> 'When two parties have come to a contract – or rather what appears on the face of it, to be a contract – the fact that one party is mistaken as to the identity of the other does not mean that there is no contract, or that the contract is a nullity and void from the beginning. It only means that the contract is voidable, that is liable to be set aside at the instance of the mistaken person so long as as he does so before third parties have in good faith acquired rights under it.'

Lord Denning had expressed a similar view in the Court of Appeal in *Gallie* v *Lee* (7) when he said: 'I have long had doubts about the theory that, in the law of contract, mistake as to the identity of the person renders a contract a nullity and void.' He went on to express reservations about the decision in *Cundy* v *Lindsay* (above). Indeed it is questionable whether that case is reconcilable with Lord Denning's formulation of the law.

The effect of holding the contract void is to prejudice the third party, who might have acted in perfect good faith. The Law Reform Committee has recommended

> '... that contracts which are at present void because the owner of the goods was deceived or mistaken as to the identity of the person with whom he dealt should in future be treated as voidable so far as third parties are concerned' (8).

If this recommendation were to be implemented by legislation it would bring a measure of certainty to this question. Admittedly it might cause hardship to owners of goods who have been deceived, but they are able to protect themselves by ensuring payment before surrendering possession of the goods: innocent third parties usually have no safeguard.

References

(1)   (1857) 2 H & N 564
(2)   (1878) 3 App Cas 459
(3)   (1897) 14 TLR 98
(4)   [1919] 2 KB 243
(5)   [1961] 1 QB 31
(6)   [1972] 1 QB 198
(7)   [1969] 2 Ch 17
(8)   12th Report (1966), Cmnd 2958, para 15

Question Eight

Les agreed to rent his lorry to Morgan for £500 per week for 104 weeks. Morgan had just started out 'on his own' and was aiming to use the lorry to transport coal to a nearby power station. After paying the agreed sum for 14 weeks Morgan fell ill and Les agreed to accept £200 per week till Morgan recovered. Morgan paid the reduced sum for the following eight weeks when Morgan's wife, Noreen, won £250,000 on her premium savings bond. Although they had agreed to share any winnings Noreen refused to share any of her prize with Morgan. Ten weeks after Noreen's win, Morgan was left £10,000 by his Uncle Oliver. Morgan continued to pay the reduced sum till in the 52nd week Les discovered what had transpired. Two weeks later Morgan made a full recovery. Les claimed the full arrears of £300 per week and requested that the lorry be returned to Les immediately. Morgan refused. At that time Les could have rented the lorry for £600 per week.

Advise Les.

Suggested Solution

General Comment

This requires discussion of the equitable doctrine of promissory estoppel. The particular issue here is whether, and to what extent, the promisor can resile from his promise.

Skeleton Solution

The common law rules with regard to the payment of a lesser sum – the origin and development of the doctrine of promissory estoppel – the operation and limits of the doctrine – the effects of the doctrine, in particular whether it is suspensive or extinctive and when it would be inequitable for the promisor to resile from his promise.

Suggested Solution

At common law the payment of a lesser sum in payment of a larger sum does not discharge the debt in the absence of consideration for the creditor abandoning the balance owing to him. This derives from the rule in *Pinnel's Case* (1), affirmed by the House of Lords in *Foakes* v *Beer* (2) and more recently by the Court of Appeal in *Re Selectmove Ltd* (3). Thus, at common law Les's promise to accept the reduced sum would be unenforceable, no consideration having been furnished for that promise, and he would be entitled to claim full implementation of Morgan's obligations.

The common law has, however, been modified by the doctrine of promissory estoppel and we are required to examine the effects of that doctrine on the rights of the parties.

The origin of the doctrine lies in the decision of the House of Lords in *Hughes* v *Metropolitan Railway Co* (4), where Lord Cairns LC stated the principle of equity that

> ' … if parties …enter upon a course of negotiation which has the effect of leading one of the parties to suppose that the strict legal rights arising under the contract will not be enforced, or will be kept in suspense, or held in abeyance, the party who otherwise might have enforced those rights will not be allowed to enforce them where it would be inequitable having regard to the dealings which have thus taken place between the parties.'

(The earlier case of *Jorden* v *Money* (5), where the House of Lords had held that estoppel related to statements of existing fact, not to promises as to the future, was not quoted.)

The equitable principle enunciated by Lord Cairns was applied by the House of Lords in the context of a landlord's claim for forfeiture of a lease. It was developed by Denning J in obiter dicta in *Central London Property Trust Ltd* v *High Trees House Ltd* (6) to extend to the payment of money. His Lordship said that 'a promise to accept a smaller sum in discharge of a larger sum, if acted upon, is binding notwithstanding the absence of consideration.'

Denning J's judgment has been criticised as being in conflict with *Foakes* v *Beer* and *Jorden* v *Money*, but the doctrine of promissory estoppel has been accepted by the courts at all levels.

It is now necessary to apply the criteria for the doctrine to operate and its effects to the facts of the present problem.

Les's promise must have been clear and unequivocal: *Woodhouse A C Israel Cocoa SA* v *Nigerian Produce Marketing Co Ltd* (7). It appears to have been so.

Morgan must have acted on the promise. It is not entirely certain what this requirement entails. It does not appear that he must have necessarily acted to his detriment. There is no clear authority, but there are obiter dicta stating that it is not necessary to show detriment: per Lord Denning MR in *W J Alan & Co Ltd* v *El Nasr Export & Import Co* (8); per Goff J in *The Post Chaser* (9). Lord Denning stated that all that is necessary is to show that the promisee must have been led to have acted differently from what he would otherwise have done. We must assume that Morgan was so led and that he acted differently by continuing with the rental of the lorry and paying the reduced sum.

That the doctrine suspends, rather than extinguishes, the promisor's rights was emphasised by the Privy Council in *F A Ajayi* v *R T Briscoe (Nigeria) Ltd* (10) and by the House of Lords in *Tool Metal Manufacturing Co Ltd* v *Tungsten Electric Co Ltd* (11). In the former case Lord Hodson said that: 'the promisor can resile from his promise on giving reasonable notice, which need not be a formal notice, giving the promisee reasonable opportunity of resuming his position'.

Les intended that his rights to the full instalments should be suspended. When he agreed that Morgan could pay the reduced sum until Morgan recovered from his illness, he must have intended that to mean until Morgan was financially able to resume payment of the full amount. Morgan's financial ability to do so is not affected by his wife Noreen's winnings. Although they had agreed to share any winnings, she has refused to do so and Morgan has no claim upon them. However, Morgan is clearly financially able to resume payment of the full instalments as from the time he received the bequest from his uncle. Les is therefore entitled to demand the resumption of the full payment of the remaining instalments.

With regard to the arrears the situation is more problematical. Is the effect of the doctrine of promissory estoppel extinctive with regard to the right to the arrears? In *High Trees* Denning J held the view that the landlord's claim for the arrear rentals would have been extinguished, but this view was unnecessary for the decision in that case as the landlord was not claiming the arrears. In the absence of authority I must submit that it is more consistent with the doctrine to hold that Les's rights to the arrears would have been extinguished, but this is subject to the equity of the situation, to which we must now turn attention.

It is central to the doctrine that the promisor will only be estopped from resiling from his promise when it would be inequitable to allow him to do so. The effect of the operation of promissory estoppel is that it raises an equity in favour of the promisee, Morgan. In this context Morgan's conduct is relevant: he failed to disclose to Les his receipt of the bequest from his uncle, and continued to pay the reduced sum for some weeks after he had received it. Does this debar him from raising the equitable defence? The only guidance we have is in the judgement of Lord Denning in *D & C Builders Ltd* v *Rees* (12). There his Lordship held that where the promise to accept the lesser sum had been obtained by a threat, by intimidation, the equity was not raised in the promisee's favour. The question is whether mere dishonesty would have the same effect. In my view it should. I conclude that on the facts presented Les would be entitled to resile completely from his promise and would also be entitled to claim the arrears.

It is, however, difficult to see on what basis Les could at this stage claim the return of the lorry. he could hardly maintain that the failure to pay the full instalments should be treated as a breach of condition which would justify termination of the contract.

References

(1)   (1602) 5 Co Rep 117a
(2)   (1864) 9 App Cas 605
(3)   [1995] 1 WLR 474
(4)   (1877) 2 App Cas 439
(5)   (1854) 5 HL Cas 185
(6)   [1947] 1 KB 130
(7)   [1972] AC 741
(8)   [1972] 2 QB 189
(9)   [1982] 1 All ER 19
(10)   [1964] 1 WLR 1326
(11)   [1955] 1 WLR 761
(12)   [1966] 2 QB 617

Law Update 2003 edition – due March 2003

An annual review of the most recent developments in specific legal subject areas, useful for law students at degree and professional levels, others with law elements in their courses and also practitioners seeking a quick update.

Published around March every year, the Law Update summarises the major legal developments during the course of the previous year. In conjunction with Old Bailey Press textbooks it gives the student a significant advantage when revising for examinations.

Contents

Administrative Law • Civil and Criminal Procedure • Commercial Law • Company Law • Conflict of Laws • Constitutional Law • Contract Law • Conveyancing • Criminal Law • Criminology • English and European Legal Systems • Equity and Trusts • European Union Law • Evidence • Family Law • Jurisprudence • Land Law • Law of International Trade • Public International Law • Revenue Law • Succession • Tort

For further information on contents or to place an order, please contact:

Mail Order
Old Bailey Press
at Holborn College
Woolwich Road
Charlton
London
SE7 8LN

Telephone No: 020 8317 6039
Fax No: 020 8317 6004
Website: www.oldbaileypress.co.uk

ISBN 1 85836 477 9
Soft cover 246 x 175 mm
450 pages approx
£10.95
Due March 2003

Unannotated Cracknell's Statutes for use in Examinations

New Editions of Cracknell's Statutes

£11.95 due 2002

Cracknell's Statutes provide a comprehensive series of essential statutory provisions for each subject. Amendments are consolidated, avoiding the need to cross-refer to amending legislation. Unannotated, they are suitable for use in examinations, and provide the precise wording of vital Acts of Parliament for the diligent student.

Commercial Law ISBN: 1 85836 472 8	**European Community Legislation** ISBN: 1 85836 470 1
Conflict of Laws ISBN: 1 85836 473 6	**Family Law** ISBN: 1 85836 471 X
Criminal Law ISBN: 1 85836 474 4	**Public International Law** ISBN: 1 85836 476 0

Employment Law
ISBN: 1 85836 475 2

For further information on contents or to place an order, please contact:

Mail Order
Old Bailey Press
at Holborn College
Woolwich Road
Charlton
London
SE7 8LN

Telephone No: 020 8317 6039
Fax No: 020 8317 6004
Website: www.oldbaileypress.co.uk

Old Bailey Press

The Old Bailey Press integrated student law library is tailor-made to help you at every stage of your studies from the preliminaries of each subject through to the final examination. The series of Textbooks, Revision WorkBooks, 150 Leading Cases and Cracknell's Statutes are interrelated to provide you with a comprehensive set of study materials.

You can buy Old Bailey Press books from your University Bookshop, your local Bookshop, direct using this form, or you can order a free catalogue of our titles from the address shown overleaf.

The following subjects each have a Textbook, 150 Leading Cases/Casebook, Revision WorkBook and Cracknell's Statutes unless otherwise stated.

Administrative Law
Commercial Law
Company Law
Conflict of Laws
Constitutional Law
Conveyancing (Textbook and 150 Leading Cases)
Criminal Law
Criminology (Textbook and Sourcebook)
Employment Law (Textbook and Cracknell's Statutes)
English and European Legal Systems
Equity and Trusts
Evidence
Family Law
Jurisprudence: The Philosophy of Law (Textbook, Sourcebook and
    Revision WorkBook)
Land: The Law of Real Property
Law of International Trade
Law of the European Union
Legal Skills and System
    (Textbook)
Obligations: Contract Law
Obligations: The Law of Tort
Public International Law
Revenue Law (Textbook,
    Revision WorkBook and
    Cracknell's Statutes)
Succession

Mail order prices:	
Textbook	£14.95
150 Leading Cases	£11.95
Revision WorkBook	£9.95
Cracknell's Statutes	£11.95
Suggested Solutions 1998–1999	£6.95
Suggested Solutions 1999–2000	£6.95
Suggested Solutions 2000–2001	£6.95
Law Update 2002	£9.95
Law Update 2003	£10.95

Please note details and prices are subject to alteration.

To complete your order, please fill in the form below:

Module	Books required	Quantity	Price	Cost
		Postage		
		TOTAL		

For Europe, add 15% postage and packing (£20 maximum).
For the rest of the world, add 40% for airmail.

ORDERING

By telephone to Mail Order at 020 8317 6039, with your credit card to hand.

By fax to 020 8317 6004 (giving your credit card details).

Website: www.oldbaileypress.co.uk

By post to: Mail Order, Old Bailey Press at Holborn College, Woolwich Road, Charlton, London, SE7 8LN.

When ordering by post, please enclose full payment by cheque or banker's draft, or complete the credit card details below. You may also order a free catalogue of our complete range of titles from this address.

We aim to despatch your books within 3 working days of receiving your order.

Name

Address

Postcode   Telephone

Total value of order, including postage: £

I enclose a cheque/banker's draft for the above sum, or

charge my   ☐ Access/Mastercard   ☐ Visa   ☐ American Express
Card number

☐☐☐☐ ☐☐☐☐ ☐☐☐☐ ☐☐☐☐

Expiry date ☐☐☐☐

Signature: ………………………………………………Date: …………………………………………